the white house

The White House has been part of Portrush since 1891. In that time it has survived two World Wars, the Great Depression and the worst of Northern Ireland's recent problems including a terrorist incendiary attack. Its history is as rich and varied as some featured in this book, from the original founder Henry Hamilton, who returned from America with an exciting vision for an emporium that would rival the best of what he had seen during his time in the States, to a period when the store was part of the Dublin based Fitzwilliam PLC, through to today. One thing that hasn't changed is the special place that the store holds for generations of visitors and locals alike.

the white house

is delighted to be the sponsor of this book, *Golden Strands*.

golden strands

Seaside Voices - Summer Tales
of Old Portrush

Maurice McAleese

*"...as a holiday destination it was said to rival
'in stir and gaiety' the leading resorts on the
other side of the channel."*

DEDICATION

For my family on the Golden Shore - my mother and father;
sister, Nan; brothers Denny, Gerald and Desmond.

Published 2009

Printed by
Impact Printing
Coleraine & Ballycastle

ISBN: 978 1 906689 14 8

contents

acknowledgements

Quoted throughout these pages are some beautifully descriptive passages from the pens of gifted reporters and writers from a century and more ago, old "voices" that conjure up memorable seaside images of Portrush in a bygone age. A few short examples: you discover the sea "dashing splendidly" against The Skerries; from a seafront cottage you hear "the sound of a harmonium, and voices singing an old hymn;" on the shore you see "the evolutions of the sea-birds, and merry bathers disporting themselves"; to the west you stumble on "a heavy little bay of sea like a tablespoon turned sideways," and, one of my favourites, "on this promontory, the terraces of Portrush shiver nakedly."

All are tributes to the quality and the character and the past glories of this special place that clings to the very tip of the north coast. For the most part they have been culled from the archives of the two local weekly newspapers, *The Constitution* and *The Chronicle,* as indeed has much of the other source material. Other references are from national newspapers, the *London Times, Daily Mail, Daily Express, Glasgow Herald*, and magazines no longer published such as *Nomad's Weekly, The Lady of the House, London Opinion* and *Land and Water.*

A selection of fine old photographs and postcards, some appearing here for the first time, considerably enhance the text. For these I have to thank Tommy McDonald and Robert Anderson, Albert Rhodich of Portrush and Margaret Campbell, Porstewart. I was pleased that I was able to include so many of my own sketches as well. There are many different strands to the book and Impact, the publishers, did a superb job in pulling them all together. I would particularly thank Freddie Bottomley, for his contribution to the design and lay-out, especially the cover.

Publication of the book was supported by an award from the North Eastern Education and Library Board through its Local Studies Scheme, and generous sponsorship was provided by The White House, one of the best known department stores in the Province. For well over a century now it has been something of an institution in Portrush and still has its own unique seaside "voice".

My aim in writing the book was to capture some of the flavour and essence of life as it was a century or so ago in the seaside history of Portrush and I hope I have managed to do this. Whether I have or not, I have enjoyed the challenge, enjoyed walking for a little while (perhaps with vagrant steps at times!) along these old, golden strands of time.

- Maurice McAleese

foreword

The period between the end of the Victorian era and the start of the Great War was the golden age of seaside holidays in Portrush; it revelled in its reputation as the undisputed "Brighton of the North" – it even had its own (though not so grand) pier.

In piecing together the "golden strands" of that mostly Edwardian period, retired journalist Maurice McAleese, who was born and brought up in Portrush, has produced a fascinating glimpse of what it was like to spend a holiday by the sea in those balmy summer days at the dawn of the twentieth century.

Prepare to be transported to an enchanting time and place. There are quite a few unexpected twists and turns along the way - and some surprising encounters with famous visitors, including a rather portly gentleman, the world's first film star, who could be found mingling with the crowds in Portrush in the summer of 1913.

This is a reverential (mostly) look at a time when Portrush, according to one source, had a Riveria atmosphere about it and the sea, on a fine day, was "as blue as the Mediterranean."

In her poem, "In Autumn," Mable V. Irvine has these opening lines:

Come, walk upon the sands
  with me;
The golden sands, the gentle
  sea
Are like a summer memory.

This book, beautifully illustrated, is an invitation to "walk upon the sands." Enjoy the walk.

Ah! what pleasant visions haunt me
As I gaze upon the sea!
All the old romantic legends,
All my dreams, come back to me.

introduction

- Henry Wadsworth Longfellow.

A hundred years ago, no less a journal than the London Times said of Portrush: "With its combination of rocky coast and great stretches of firm sand, it is a charming watering-place, with a truly magnificent outlook seawards to where the Skerries lie, a natural breakwater against which the sea, when it is high, dashes splendidly."

The Times also noted that Portrush had a very good hotel built by the Northern Counties Railway, now owned by the Midland Railway of England, and it also had one of the best golf courses in the British Islands.

At about the same time, it was also reported that His Excellency the Buvaraja of Mysore "and his suite" had paid a visit to Portrush and the Giant's Causeway and had been overnight guests in the hotel.

In those days, one of the outstanding features and attractions of the hotel was its magnificent ballroom and the regular Saturday night dances were very well patronised. According to an old pamphlet, "the grand ballroom, when brilliantly lighted, as it is on these occasions, presents as bright and alluring a moving picture as one could well wish to see. The floor is always in the pink of condition, and excellent music is supplied by a band from Derry and several very large parties have been catered for this season." Plenty of glitz and glamour in surroundings of style and elegance to boot, so let's hope His Excellency the Buvaraja was suitably impressed!

His visit was in the summer of 1913. It was a good time to spend a holiday in Portrush because from almost every angle it was a record-breaking season, not least weather-wise – for most of July and August and a good part of September the sun had shone almost continuously out of a cloudless sky. Thus it was recorded "…it may now be said that the most successful season on record has come to an end. This is the opinion of the great majority of the merchants, hotel and boarding-house owners, and others whose incomes are more or less affected by the summer visitors."

Portrush was on the crest of a golden wave. In a Dublin magazine called "The Lady of the House," it was described as "the most fashionable marine resort in Ulster, and nearest to that natural and awe-inspiring wonder, the Giant's Causeway." Rather caustically, the writer added that it was humiliating to reflect that "the merits of the Antrim coast scenery are more widely appreciated by Englishmen than by Irishmen born out of Ulster, that probably twenty people come from the other side of the Channel for the one who journeys up to Belfast and the Causeway from the southern and midland counties of Ireland."

The town is mentioned in the 1908 edition of Porter's Directory as "rapidly rising in the estimation of the British public as a watering-place and pleasure resort, every succeeding year bringing an increasing number of visitors and is generally recognised as the Queen of Irish seaside resorts."

The entry went on to state that Turkish, hot, cold and sea water baths "abound" and that theatres, entertainments and amusements of all kinds were up to the standard of any English or Continental resort. "Hotels are thoroughly up to date and furnished or unfurnished houses and apartments can be had at most reasonable charges."

In the course of just one July day in 1913, no fewer than 70 trains arrived at "the Port". Coping with such large numbers of passengers, far from being the nightmare you might think, was a smooth operation, thanks in large measure to Mr. Michael Keenan. He was the very efficient Stationmaster at Portrush and so well organised were he and his staff that there was "very little congestion."

However, the arrival of just two ladies by train on one occasion and the rather amusing episode that ensued must have caused the highly efficient Mr Keenan a few anxious moments. The ladies, both Americans, arrived on the 3pm train from Belfast and they were instantly assailed by a crowd of hotel porters. Four or five porters grabbed hold of their luggage while others surrounded them, holding up cards from a variety of establishments. The ladies were slightly embarrassed but it all ended amicably when at length they decided on the Londonderry Hotel "and the smiling porter strutted off with the luggage under his arms, followed by the envious eyes of his disappointed confreres."

The summer of that year was so good that it was described by one travel writer as an "annas mirabilis" so far as seaside holidays in Northern Ireland were concerned and he pointed out that along the whole of the northern coastline there was not an empty house.

Full steam ahead at the Arcadia

In August, an item in the local Press noted: "In these days everybody is on the move – if possible to the seaside. All trains bound for the sea are filled with happy passengers and the resorts on the northern coast have rarely contained so many visitors as they do at the present time. There is still, of course, room for more; but it is, we opine, the general opinion of merchants and residents from Castlerock to Cushendall that as regards public patronage our watering-places have this month reached high-water mark."

A nice image of what it was like to spend a holiday at the seaside one hundred years ago is conjured up in this extract from a magazine article about Portrush: "All day long visitors are dipping in the deliciously cool pools, with their blended tints of indigo, brown and green; whilst along its golden strands long straggling lines of children and grown-ups are seen at all hours of the day wading and paddling in the endless fringe of unsullied wavelets, coming in too gently, too softly, to tip their crests with spray."

So popular was Portrush as a holiday destination that it was said to rival "in stir and gaiety" the leading resorts on the other side of the Channel. This from a newspaper article: "In the thronged streets, across the green undulations of the golf links, on the golden sands, and even in the blue sea, the accents of bonnie Scotland are heard, and often far into the balmy night the strains of 'Annie Laurie' or some other favourite Scottish air reach the ear."

That was not too surprising, perhaps, because a cross-Channel ferry service operated between Portrush and Ardrossan and there were daily sailings throughout the summer season – in the months of July and August in 1913 it was estimated that the steamers conveyed some 25,000 passengers to and from Portrush. That summer there had been an enormous influx of visitors from Scotland. A writer in the Glasgow Herald highlighted the fact that there had been a great exodus from the West of Scotland, something he believed was "doubtless due to the spell of good trade, which provided the wherewithal, and the lure of the weather, which promised admirable conditions for a trip to coast or country."

A busy day at the West Strand

Another barometer of what seems to have been a truly remarkable season in the north coast resort was highlighted in this way: "...the absence, for long periods of the day, of hackney cars at the Station Square, is indicative of good business among the jarvies."

The jaunting-car was a familiar sight on the streets and the owners were enjoying a good season but they were beginning to voice concern at the growing number of motor-cars, some of them for hire, which were starting to adversely affect their trade. Perhaps they realised that the age of the motor-car had arrived and that horse-power of a different kind would soon take over.

Thanks to a visitor to Portrush at the beginning of the last century, a man called Harold Begbie, we have a tantalising and atmospheric glimpse into what it was like to be beside the seaside in those old days. He wrote a lengthy and glowing article about Portrush and it appeared in the Daily Mail. This is just a small extract: "…the place still has the charm of an ancient fishing village. Step from your hotel at night – heavily cloaked in autumn – and at the first pace or two you are away from the spirit and atmosphere of convenient luxury. Against the dim-lit window of a toy and sweet shop a bunch of barefoot boys press their noses and exchange desires. A young sailor stands on the doorstep whispering to a girl with a shawl about her head. From one of the cottages comes the sound of a harmonium, and voices singing an old hymn. At the windy corner, five or six ancient mariners, smoking pipes as if the tobacco were a question seriously to be debated, stand like figures carved out of rock, their muffled voices sounding like echoes soughing through a cave."

Perhaps Mr. Begbie was being a little too romantic in his description of barefoot boys and ancient mariners. However, to describe this period as the golden age of seaside holidays in Portrush, would not be an exaggeration. Another golden age, I like to think, was when I was growing up there some three decades or so later, because what I remember is balmy summers filled with warm sunny days, the sound and swirl of the sea, the soft white sands, streets of boarding-houses full of guests, particularly my mother's boarding house in Causeway Street, the buzz of visitors in every part of the town and the clamour of the old Giant's Causeway tram as it trundled past our front door. Yes, I think it may well have been a golden age too. Anyway, the memories I have are all tinged with gold.

The s.s.Melmore entering Portrush Harbour.
From a painting by R.D.Beattie

MAURICE McALEESE

call of the sea

"...the broad sun is sinking down in its tranquillity;
the gentleness of heaven is on the sea."

The simple beauty of those lines in Wordsworth's poem, "By the Sea,"
resonates with me, probably because I have always lived close to the
sea, and I know it in all its moods; but I like its "gentleness of heaven"
best of all.

So I'm going to take you on a magical, mystical journey to golden (and
mostly gentle) wave-washed shores and quiet island roads where seabirds
wheel and dance on the ocean breeze; where soft, wind-rippled sand
conceals the footprints of time and tide and sun-dappled waves whisper.

Down by the harbour wall we'll meet the old fishermen who sit and dream,
listening to the soft sea voices, sailing away, on memories tides, to old,
familiar ports, their dreams, like their hard lives, the sad echo of a restless
longing.

On the journey there will be echoes, too, of style and elegance, beauty and
opulence, in lives played out majestically against the gentle sea rhythms;
and lives of quiet heroism, unsung and largely forgotten, shrouded in old
sea mists. They helped to shape this special place, bestowing upon it,
when the twentieth century was young, a royal status - "Queen" of
Ireland's seaside resorts.

Don't be put off when I tell you that on this journey we will not be travelling
too far from the town of Portrush, because it will be a journey with a
difference, a journey on time's winged chariot, taking us back to a very

different place from the one you might know today. Hopefully, for a little while, we will be able to stroll on golden strands and savour the sights and the sounds, the pleasures and delights of old summer days at the seaside.

"In these delightful days and nights one's fancy longingly turns to thoughts of the seaside, with its crisp, cooling breezes and the dancing of its sunny wavelets along the yellow sand and among the low-lying rocks, whither old folks from the rural districts are wont to repair in quiet hours, there to sit in silent joy, dangling bare feet in the weedy pools."

Portrush was definitely a much more lively and vibrant place than the image conjured up in those lines by a writer at the beginning of the last century. The minstrel-going public of 1904, another seaside writer noted, were in for a treat when Billy Keene "and his merry boys and girls" would shortly make their first appearance of the season. Mr. Keene had secured the leading position on the Pleasure Grounds at the Railway Station, where he had already pitched his moving pavilion, equipped with acetylene light and all the paraphernalia pertaining to his alfresco entertainments.

So let's start with a little whistle-stop tour of the town and if we're lucky, we could meet not only Mr. Keene, but also Prime Ministers and First Lords of the Admiralty (complete with golf clubs), world-famous entertainers, including a very special star of the silver screen, the world's first film star, in fact. We'll also meet a young girl, from Australia, who took a dip in the harbour shortly after she had

made swimming history at the 1912 Olympic Games in Stockholm – and nobody realised who she was!

We're just outside the smart Tudor style railway station now, one of the finest in the country and a landmark building - later, if we've time, we'll go inside and we'll see what surely must be the world's largest grandfather clock – it's 18 feet tall and part of the fabric and the style and the grandeur, not to mention old world charm, of this distinctive building.

The station is a busy place just now because it's the height of the holiday season – even so, you'll probably be as surprised as I was to learn that in the space of just one day last week, for example, no fewer than 70 special trains brought thousands of visitors and excursionists to the town. Now that's busy!

That's the Causeway tram parked just outside the railway station – it's where the eight mile journey to and from the Giant's Causeway begins and ends. And we're in luck today. The distinguished looking gentleman standing at the front of the tram talking to the driver is William Acheson Traill the brilliant engineer whose genius and ambition gave Portrush this jewel in the crown - the world's first hydro-electric tramway. Perhaps this afternoon we'll take a trip to the Causeway – the journey usually takes about 40 minutes.

W.A. TRAILL, C.E.

Pioneer of hydro-electric traction and founder of the Giant's Causeway electric tramway

1844-1933

Now, though, we'll head down Kerr Street towards the harbour, another busy hub of activity throughout the summer months mainly due to the daylight passenger steamship service between Portrush and Ardrossan. I see that one of the ships, probably the Hazel, has just docked, because the jarvies are all down there waiting for the passengers to disembark. There are a few motor-cars, or taxis, as well although it's a little more expensive to travel in them. It's amazing to think that the Hazel can carry upwards of a thousand passengers and at this time of the year she always seems to have a full complement.

Did you notice a group of people over there on that grassy mound overlooking the harbour watching an artist painting a picture of the busy scene? You'll never guess who the artist is - none other than Percy French, the great songwriter and entertainer. He comes to Portrush regularly during the summer. Most people know he wrote the famous song, "The Mountains of Mourne," and many others, but not many realise that as well as a songwriter he is also a very accomplished artist. Most likely he will be appearing at the Picture Palace, providing entertainment during intervals between the film shows. Incidentally, the Picture Palace is housed in the Town Hall, that big red brick building opposite the railway station.

We passed it on the way down to the harbour and we also passed the Pavilion, near the railway station, a really popular venue for dancing, skating and variety shows and it also has a picture house. It contains three large halls, in fact, each capable of accommodating a thousand people. Remarkable, isn't it?

We've encountered Percy French today in Portrush. We must also keep an eye out for Harry Lauder, the great Scottish entertainer, also a regular here, and he must feel quite at home among the many thousands of his fellow countrymen who visit during the various Scottish fair holiday periods. We could also run into John Bunny, a very famous American comedy actor of the silent screen – some say he was the world's first film-star. I'm told he's in town at present. He was seen strolling unassumingly along the seafront the other day so maybe, if he's still here, we'll be able to catch up with him.

By the way, watch out for the water-cart, because you might get a bit of a soaking! Water from the horse-drawn cart is sprayed on the streets regularly, particularly if it's a little bit windy, to keep down the blowing sand and dust and if you happen to be in the way…The water they use is drawn from the sea, so there's no danger of a shortage!

We're coming to the lower end of Main Street now and the Lansdowne area and as you can see there's quite a lot of activity going on here too. If Portrush had a casino, I suppose it would be located somewhere in this part of the town. Instead, it has the next best (or worst) thing – gambling tables set up on the street and in other open spaces. The roulette table seems to be the most popular. Not all of the townspeople are happy about the gambling tables because occasionally there are disturbances, but I suppose if you're on holiday, a little flutter now and again seems harmless enough.

Now we've arrived at Lansdowne. That building right on the edge of the sea is the lifeboat house. As you know, Portrush has a proud tradition as a lifeboat station and the launching of the lifeboat is a spectacle worth seeing. In the summer it's launched regularly as a fund-raising exercise so hopefully we'll be able to attend one of these in the next day or two.

Next to the lifeboat station is the small Portandoo harbour where some of the local fishermen operate boat trips to the Skerry Islands a couple of miles out. If the weather is good and the sea is calm enough, it's possible to disembark and many trippers spend a pleasant time having a picnic there. From the shore, it doesn't seem possible because of the sloping nature of the rocks but there you go. One of the boatmen told me that the local fire brigade once held their annual sports day on the Skerries!

From here we can see the Blue Pool, one of the main venues for swimming and diving displays and water carnivals that are so popular with summer visitors. There are some really good divers in Portrush and they always give stunning and spectacular exhibitions, especially from the high diving board. There are some accomplished lady divers and they take part in the displays alongside the men but ordinarily they are not allowed to bathe here – it's strictly reserved for male swimmers, which is rather strange because so-called "mixed" bathing is allowed at the other popular diving and swimming venue, the South Pier at the harbour.

We're not too far away now from the Arcadia which has a small beach and this is called the Ladies Bathing Place, so the ladies also have an exclusive bathing area. That nice building overlooking the beach is the Arcadia Café and it's here each summer that Madame Levante and her ladies band entertain customers and put on special concerts. I think it must be one of the few ladies bands in the country and they are certainly an attraction for many people in Portrush.

The broad sweep of the East Strand is just ahead and it's here that perhaps the most familiar seaside image is provided by a man called Henry Ireland. Each summer his ponies, horses and donkeys provide great entertainment for children and grown-ups alike. At the other end of the East Strand is the White Rocks with its stunning backdrop of cliffs and caves. It's one of the most popular venues for picnics.

For now, that's just a little portrait of Portrush as it might have been on any one of a number of bright summer days in the early part of the last century when it was a mecca for thousands of holidaymakers "dancing like a wave upon the shore."

grocers, golfers and grumblers

- MAURICE McALEESE -

A writer extolling the virtues of a holiday in Portrush in the early part of the last century proclaimed: "Wherever your vagrant steps wander in the vicinity of Portrush, the sea is never far away. It is a perpetual attraction, and visitors from inland towns are constantly fascinated by the flap and churn of the Atlantic rollers, the evolutions of the sea-birds, and the merry bathers disporting themselves…"

He was writing about the many fine walks near Portrush and in this piece he was concentrating particularly on Dunluce Castle, situated about three miles from the town. It could be reached, he suggested, by means of the electric tram, or by walking along the East Strand, and ascending to the road at the White Rocks.

In this way he was making the subtle point that the past also contributed something, as he put it, "to the quiet rest of seaside life." The grey shell of Dunluce spoke of the "vanished glories of the McQuillans and the McDonnells" and the winds of fable, he wrote, were constantly blowing across the Giant's Causeway. The seaside was a place where past and present alike came to the visitor's aid… and the quiet, and the rest, and the song of the sea, was good for the soul as well as the body.

> "It was but a little while ago that Portrush lay in my dreams as Heaven in miniature…"
>
> - from an article in the Manchester Daily Despatch.

That may have been overstating the case somewhat because at the height of the holiday season Portrush was anything but quiet, particularly when it was full of Scottish holidaymakers who knew how to enjoy themselves and probably didn't know, or very much care, about past and present coming to their aid! In a newspaper article from roughly the same time, "the gaiety of the streets, especially at weekends" was mentioned; so many visitors had come to Portrush that it would not be possible to cram many more in "without a danger of them overflowing into the sea or falling over Ramore cliffs."

That old article, entitled, "The Rush to Portrush" (the author was not named) went on to give a fascinating picture-postcard profile of the resort: "The incoming trains are exceedingly well filled, never were so many motor-driven vehicles seen here, all bent on pleasure, and the streets and bathing places are bright and merry as a carnival. The picture-houses have no appearance of waning, nor does the Terrace or Ramore Hill call out in vain for paraders."

It was a time of change, particularly with regard to transport, and although there were still plenty of jaunting-cars on the streets of Portrush, there were also motor-cars for hire. Char-a-bancs could be seen "daily speeding along the coast, east and west, yielding health and joy to their crowded passengers."

En route to the Causeway

As yet, they did not pose any threat to the electric tram which "circulated" many times a day to and from the Giant's Causeway, "not infrequently loaded with sightseers from far and near."

It was noted also that there had been a significant increase in the number of southern people coming to Portrush to enjoy its magnificent sea, strands and cliffs and they were "flourishing wonderfully in its tonic and stimulating air."

About a decade earlier, in August, 1901, the Manchester Daily Despatch carried a news feature which also gave a fascinating description of Portrush. This is the stunning opening sentence: "It was but a little while ago that Portrush lay in my dreams as Heaven in miniature..."

Nature, the writer was convinced, had drawn up the plan of the place "in a more than commonly felicitous moment." With more swaggering turns of phrase, this is how the peninsular shape of Portrush was described: "Not three furlongs before sidling into Derry, the County of Antrim drops a stout forearm of rock and sand into the open Atlantic. On this promontory the terraces of Portrush shiver nakedly."

The purple prose continues when he comes to the West Bay, "a bend of strand and hill, pulled up short by a rough cliff of basalt, where it receives a heavy little bay of sea like a tablespoon turned sideways."

That same summer, a contributor to "a Belfast paper" took a more irreverent look at Portrush and rather surprisingly, perhaps, it was reprinted in The Constitution, the local weekly. The introduction is calm enough: "From a small fishing village, like that which is usually portrayed in the parish almanac (two houses, two boats on the beach, two be-whiskered sailor men, one dog and a female carrying a basket) it has in a comparatively few years leaped into the front rank of popularity as a high class watering-place."

After the calm the storm: "It has palatial hotels, so very exclusive that unless you are accompanied by a bag of golf clubs, can trace your ancestry back for at least three centuries, and prove that the blue blood in your veins is a natural product, you have a very poor chance of being allowed to pay the very high prices they demand for the privilege of breathing inside."

The storm abates and readers are assured there are many other hotels which are much less demanding and the writer goes on to assert as positive proof of its greatness the fact that Portrush has developed "the Isle of Man" style of boarding-house very successfully. This, it was contended, was always a true sign that a seaside resort had reached the high water-mark of popularity – the boarding-house with inclusive terms – the sort of place where you lost your money if you missed a meal.

Bargain breaks and budget holidays were still a long way off, nevertheless there were plenty of holidaymakers in search of a bargain: "In July or August it is an education to watch the little parties of tin-trunk tourists meandering from door to door in search of apartments at something below the regular charge. If they are unsuccessful they have not the slightest objection to camping out on the sands, but never for one moment do they relax the death-like grip on the little box which seems to contain all their earthly possessions."

The Portrush barmaids had impressed this writer greatly; apparently they possessed a unique style and character, wearing the latest Parisian creations and "performing their duties in a delightfully dreamy way, as if every graceful movement had only been perfected after years of patient practice."

In those days Portrush had, apparently, a very Continental and cosmopolitan air about it: "The hotel waiters are German, the barmaids are Cockney, the bulk of the visitors are American, and the balance of the population is made up of grocers, golfers and grumblers. When you chance to hear an American dandy asking a Cockney barmaid for a 'cocktail' and watch both faces when she informs him that she has only whiskey or stout, you will have a study worth reproducing."

Rather surprisingly, Portrush did not have any public toilets in those early days. Although the Urban Council had considered providing them on numerous occasions, nothing was done about it until the summer of 1914 when the first public toilets appeared, one of them on a site beside the Town Hall. At a Council meeting towards the end of the previous year the subject had been debated once again and the feeling was that Portrush was lagging behind other resorts in this regard. That point struck home and this time the Council resolved to do something about it.

Was Portrush really a town of grocers, golfers and grumblers? There's probably a gem of truth in there somewhere – The Derry and Antrim Year Book for that time lists 15 grocers shops in Portrush . Perhaps that is what inspired a local scribe to pen this very clever and amusing little ditty entitled "The Grocer"

A grocer loved a charming girl,
As lovely as the day;
He wondered if she'd marry him,
And said "Let's Soap she may."

And straight to her house he went,
Her lovely face to see,
Exclaiming "Ah, I know full well
That Cheese the girl for me."

The girl was very kind, and said
That she was very glad
To see him there, and then remarked,
What a bad Coffee had.

And soon they got most intimate –
She let him kiss her brow;
But when he spoke of marriage, said,
"Oh do not Teas me now."

The grocer's spirits fell at this,
He felt as though he'd die,
And hinted at a suicide,
While she Bacon to cry.

"You silly boy, you don't suppose
I'm blind to all your merits."
It's evident she knew a way
Of Raisin up his spirits.

But true love's course did ne'er run smooth,
Her father saw them kiss;
And kicked him from the room, and said,
"You Biscuit out of this."

"Oh, father, you are cruel, to
So roughly handle us;"
Thus spoke the girl, and father said:
"I think its Candle us."

Papa relented when he saw
His child begin to cry;
"There, there, you think my treatment harsh,
My daughter, Soda I."

"There, keep your lover, dry your eyes,
And let's have no more row;
I did not like the man, but my
Opinion Salt erd now."

The two were wed, and made a pair,
By no means ill assorted,
And happy ever after were,
It's Current ly reported.

I suppose you could say that in composing that little tome the writer used very Flour ey language!

Hopefully it was worth making that little grocery detour. On a more serious note, there was little doubt that Portrush was a place where drooping spirits could be easily revived by the sights and sounds of the sea, not to mention those "merry bathers disporting themselves."

"...the placid joy of bright coloured knots of men and women scattered along the green slopes of Ramore Hill."

seaside "census"

A n unusual "census" took place in Portrush in the early part of the last century. It was not really a census in the strict sense of the word, more a survey, and it was mainly targeted at tourists – the object of the exercise was to establish just how many visitors were coming to Portrush at the height of the holiday season, something which, until then, had been simply based on estimates. So in the summer of 1911 this so-called census, completely unofficial and probably the first of its kind in any seaside resort in the Province, was conducted with a view to ascertaining the number of visitors staying in Portrush on the night of August 13.

No one was excluded – residents were also counted – and the results showed that on that particular night the population of Portrush was almost four times greater – 8,033 compared with the normal or winter population of 2,280.

The undertaking was down to an enterprising piece of local journalism because the whole thing was planned and organised by the local weekly newspaper, *The Constitution*, then acknowledged as the leading weekly in the Province.

An editorial explained: "Shrewd guesses are often made as to the number of visitors in Portrush during the height of the season, but no precise data has hitherto been available for testing how far these idle conjectures approach to accuracy. It is exceedingly important, for several obvious reasons, that we and the catering public should know how many visitors have to be fed and accommodated and, if possible, entertained during the summer months."

And with a little bit of trumpet-blowing, the editorial writer continued: "The Constitution has now placed this important matter beyond doubt or conjecture. It sent into the township on Monday last a band of enumerators, properly instructed, and a complete census was taken of the number of residents and visitors – men, women and children – who slept in Portrush on the night of Sunday last, August 13, 1911."

A nice little pen picture of what seaside holidays were like one hundred years ago was painted in an article announcing the findings of the survey. This is the introduction: "No one can walk through the thronged streets of Portrush at the present time, or look upon the groups of merry bathers in the shining water, or watch the activity of juveniles digging caves in the sand or building structures of strange design, or admire the placid joy of bright coloured knots of men and women scattered along the green slopes of Ramore Hill – most of the young ones immersed in the romantic intricacies of the latest sixpenny novels – without feeling that the universal craving for the cool breezes of the seaside is being to a large extent satisfied." Phew!

Surf Bathing at Portrush

That splendid piece of prose says it all, and not in a nutshell!

Apparently there was a bit of a heatwave in the Province at the time; according to the Constitution "the sun is blazing from a cloudless sky and the heat is intolerable in the stifling city. Everyone longs for the balmy wind that comes so gratefully over the salt water and the swish of the tide on the wet strand."

These sultry days, The Constitution further commented, "have driven everybody to the seashore who can afford to get there. As a consequence, all the seaside resorts are unusually crowded. It takes a good many visitors to fill Portrush nowadays, but at the weekend the ever popular resort was filled literally to overflowing. "The results of the historic survey showed that the total population of the urban district of Portrush was 7,458 but, as The

Constitution pointed out "if we deduct from this figure the number of residents (as ascertained on 1st April last) namely, 2,150, the total number of visitors in the urban district will be found to be 5,308. More than 1,000 persons slept in the various hotels and the principal boarding-houses in the town."

It was explained that the population of Dhu Varren area on the outskirts of the town, and other dwelling houses just outside the present urban district, amounted to 1,575, making a grand total of residents and visitors in the whole area of 8,033. By deducting the resident population (2,230) the grand total was reduced to 5,753 which was the total number of visitors sleeping in Portrush and immediate neighbourhood.

The findings were no doubt of great benefit to those engaged in the tourist industry in Portrush – it was noted that more than 1,000 persons had slept in the various hotels and the three principal boarding-houses in the town – and hopefully it helped to point the way ahead for the benefit not only of holidaymakers but also of the townspeople. No effort appears to have been made to ascertain just where the holidaymakers were coming from, the enumerators confining themselves to the single question of accommodation.

For the record, the street by street summer population figures were given as follows: Salisbury Terrace, 201; Golf Terrace, 355; Eglinton Street, 261; Kerr Street and Quarry Court, 576; Mark Street, 522; Mount Royal, Main Street and Atlantic Avenue, 1,646; Bath Street, 134; Princess Terrace, 448; Lansdowne Crescent, 603.

Bazaar Street and Garden Court, 210; The Quay, 26; Bath Terrace, 321; Seabank, Dunluce Villas, Seacourt, 275; Causeway Street, 1,329; Dunluce Street, Eglinton Avenue and Sandy Row, 197; Victoria Street, 247; Craigvara Terrace, 41; Croc-na-mac Road, 66; Dhu Varren and Coleraine Road, 371; Cloughorr and Ballywillan Road, 204.

The Constitution must have had a special interest in tourism because it quite regularly published extensive lists of holidaymakers – names and where they came from and which hotel or boarding-house they were staying in. Street by street, and almost house by house because there was a large number of boarding and guest-houses then, the paper published the details and it took up quite a lot of space, spreading into a second page sometimes.

Just why this was done is not clear unless it was meant to boost circulation but I don't think people on holiday would have bought the local paper just to see their names in print. However, that's only my opinion and who knows, maybe it did help to sell a few more copies.

"...Portrush is recommended by physicians for its pure, dry and bracing climate."

24 hotels - and fully booked

Today you could count the number of hotels in Portrush on the fingers of one hand. It was a different story 100 years ago. A directory for 1908 lists Portrush as having no fewer than 24 hotels!

So just for the record, these are the hotels: Alexandria, Lansdowne Crescent – Proprietors, Mrs Dunseath and Miss Dobbin; Central, Messrs Hamilton & Co; City, Miss McConaghy, manageress; Coolnagee, Messrs Hamilton & Co; Eglinton, J. Gibb, manager; Golf, Miss McCrea, proprietress; Hamilton's, Coolnagee; Imperial, P. McKenna, proprietor; Lancashire Temperance, Mrs Taylor; Lansdowne Hotel & The Tower House, Lee & Co, proprietors; Leek's Portrush Hotel; Lismara, Lansdowne Crescent, H.A.G. Black, proprietor; Lloyd's Commercial Temperance, Kerr Street; Londonderry, Main Street, W. Markland, proprietor.

Metropole, J. Elcot, manager; Meyola Private Hotel, Mark Street, Miss Donaghy, proprietress; Northern Counties, F. Oddinwood, manager; Osborne, Mrs Hurst, proprietress; Royal, Lansdowne Crescent, Miss Dunn, proprietress; Railway, P. Bradley, proprietor; Ramore, Mr. McNally; The Esplanade, Bath Terrace, Misses Hill, proprietors; Windsor, Messrs Hamilton & Co; York, Mrs Watt.

The Northern Counties was the largest and certainly one of the best hotels and over the busy summer months it catered for large numbers of guests. So what was it like in those days? This description is taken from an advertisement in an old guide book:

"This magnificent hotel, one of the largest and best in Ireland, is under Railway management. Table d'Hote Breakfast, Luncheon and Dinner. Hot and Cold Salt Water Bathing and Posting Establishments in connection with

Hotel. The latter provides carriages, cars, etc., for the Causeway, Dunluce Castle and other places of interest at moderate charges. Portrush, the starting point for the famous Antrim Coast Route, is beautifully situated, and is recommended by physicians for its pure, dry and bracing climate. Tariff sent on application."

In April, 1912 it was announced that the seawater baths, long associated with the hotel, had been removed and the long range of buildings in which they were housed, was now being utilised as a motor garage, coach-house and stables. It was noted in the local Press: "Keen disappointment is felt at the removal of the baths, but we learn that the public will be admitted to the fine baths contained in the hotel, at specified hours, on payment of a small fee, so the loss is more imaginary than real."

It was just one illustration of the role played by the hotel in relation to the welfare and well-being of the citizens of Portrush. On another occasion, when the Urban Council was finding it difficult to raise funds to hire a band for the summer season, the hotel management stepped in and offered to pay half of the cost. Admittedly, this was in return for an arrangement whereby the band would play on the green in front of the hotel once a day. The Council gratefully accepted the offer because the band was still able to play at three or four other locations in the town. Also, when the Council was searching for suitable premises to entertain a large party of sailors from a visiting warship, again the hotel came to the rescue, offering the spacious Station Café which was owned by the company.

A book could be written about the Northern Counties Hotel on its own, with its stunning ballroom, swimming pool and no doubt an amazing list of distinguished guests down through the years. And of course its destruction in a devastating fire in 1990.

In those busy summers of a century ago, any kind of accommodation in Portrush was sometimes hard to come by. A report from July, 1913 put it like this: "Just now Portrush is donning its best aspect so far as animation is concerned, and when the Glasgow Fair people have all arrived, the accommodation in the boarding-houses and hotels will be taxed to its fullest capacity."

For visitors to Portrush in those heady summer days there was also an offer of hotel accommodation which included free transport on the famous old Causeway tram. The Causeway Hotel "charmingly situated" on the headland in close proximity to the Giant's Causeway, was advertising the fact that visitors to the hotel would be carried free on the tramway from

Portrush by asking the conductor for coupons on payment of their tram fare, which would be refunded at the Hotel office.

The Causeway Hotel was anxious to assure clients that it had "a widespread reputation for its unique location, its unsurpassed scenery, its equable climate and invigorating Atlantic breezes for those in quest of health or pleasure." The hotel's charges were moderate, the comfort undeniable and the cuisine excellent. An advertisement in the local Press also gave the

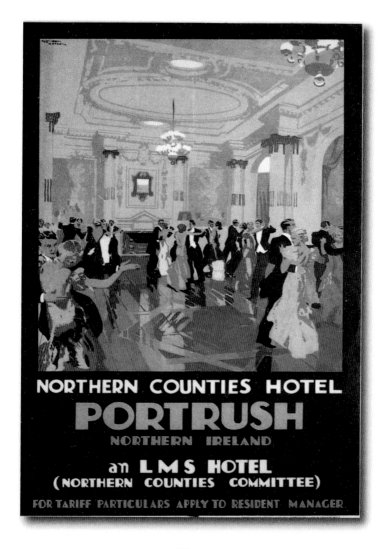

following information: "The Electric Tramway conveys visitors direct from the Railway Station at Portrush to the Causeway."

It was a good package deal because it also included, for weekly visitors, free admission coupons to the Causeway and as well as the trams there were also char-a-banc runs daily from the hotel to Carrick-a-Rede. The advertisement concluded with this warning: "Do not be misled by interested parties giving false representations regarding the hotel."

The Causeway Hotel had competition right on its doorstep because Kane's Royal Hotel, "where the traveller will find a home from home" was situated close by. An old advertisement sets out the tariff as follows: Tea, from sixpence to one shilling; Lunch, from one shilling to two shillings; Dinner, from one shilling and sixpence to two shillings and sixpence. Bedrooms for one person from two shillings; for two persons, from three shillings. And in black type, prospective guests were warned to keep to the right on leaving the trams, and insist on getting to Kane's.

The author of an article published in Dublin's "Lady of the House" magazine wrote: "Arrived at the Causeway, Mrs Kane will be prepared to welcome the traveller to her homely establishment, the Royal Hotel, and to look after one's personal wants with the assiduity that recalls the olden times when the master of the inn gave his personal attention to each and every individual guest."

Most of the Scottish visitors, of course, had pre-booked their accommodation but quite a few, it seems, did not and at busy times this posed quite a problem and sometimes it meant having to go to neighbouring resorts such as Portstewart or Castlerock.

One Scottish visitor was so impressed with his accommodation that when he returned home he wrote a letter to the editor of the Glasgow Herald. He had stayed in the house in Portrush which was at one time occupied by Sir Walter Scott, namely, Ramore House, close to Ramore Hill. In the letter he pointed out that Scott had visited Portrush in 1814 and was received by Dr. Richardson, the man who had been responsible for cultivating a new variety of florin grass. Scott had been shown over Dunluce Castle in the course of his trip. However, he had not been too impressed with Portrush; he wrote in his diary that he detested the recollection of the place as it was while he was there that he first heard of the death of his friend, the Duchess of Buccleuch.

It was not only hotels and boarding-houses which provided accommodation for the visitors – camping out was becoming an attractive option for many.

"Portrush seems to be growing in popularity as a camping out ground," it was reported. "The sandhills, particularly that portion between the railway embankment and the East Strand, are studded with tents. Early on Thursday morning some fourteen additional tents were pitched, and later in the day were taken possession of by First and Second Derry and First Omagh Companies of the Boys' Brigade."

Accommodation was also a problem on another occasion when one of the passenger steamships arrived in Portrush from Ardrossan shortly after two o'clock in the morning with about 600 passengers on board. It was reported that "...notwithstanding the inhospitable hour, lines of jaunting cars were waiting, and long before dawn a large proportion of the visitors were being whirled away to various destinations in the country districts, while the remainder found temporary homes in Portrush, or courted sleep on the sand dunes by the shore. Fortunately the weather was delightful, and sleeping out under the pearly canopy of the early morning, so far from being a hardship, was indeed a pleasure and a privilege to dwellers in the congested and dingy city." Hopefully, they did not have to spend the remainder of their holiday under the pearly canopy no matter how pleasant the experience.

Everything in the garden was not all rosy in Portrush in those days because, surprisingly, there were no public toilets anywhere in the town! So perhaps it was just as well that there were so many hotels. Presumably quite a lot of visitors would have been nipping in and out of hotels and cafes and pubs simply to use the bathroom. The first public toilet did not materialise until 1914 when one was built on a site adjacent to the Town Hall.

Although it belongs to an earlier time in the history of Portrush as a seaside resort, it's being included here because of the delightfully quaint and expressive language used by a very persuasive guest house proprietor determined to drum up business. This is how he made his pitch in an advertisement dating from 1761:

"At the house commonly called 'Bushfoot', where John Dunkins esq. usually lived, there will be lodgers kept for bathers or for those who have a mind to drink the salt water, by Edward Fayth. Any gentlemen or ladies who will favour him with their company may depend on clean and orderly attendance with a reasonable charge, his wife being an Englishwoman. Also he will keep a cakehouse for those who pass by on way to the Giant's Causeway, with cider and mead, and a fish dinner will be dressed for any that incline to dine, and those who come to bathe are desired to give a week's warning to your most obedient, humble servant, Edward Fayth. N.B. He intends the keeping of goats."

MAURICE McALEESE

promiscuous promenading

Portrush must surely occupy a unique position in the annals of railway history, not for any kind of laudable record or achievement, although there were a few of those - when the railway station was opened in the mid-nineteenth century the general opinion was that it was one of the finest and most handsome buildings in the country. However, it must surely be the only railway station from which members of the public were banned. This followed a decision by the Belfast and Northern Counties Railway Company at the beginning of the last century. The ban came into force on 1st May, 1903 but it did not mean that Portrush became a "ghost station" – the trains were still arriving and departing as normal and passengers were not inconvenienced in any way.

So what was going on? No doubt there was an official announcement of some kind but the reference I have is from a news report of the time. It states: "We are informed that the Belfast and Northern Counties Railway Company have decided that from 1st May the railway station will be closed to the public. This, we understand, will not in any way interfere with the liberty of a friend seeing a passenger off by train, to enter upon the railway premises, but is intended as a check to the promiscuous promenading of the platforms which has hitherto impeded passenger traffic, and of which many complaints have been made. It is a step that will be commended by the travelling public."

" "The scenes at the station, before the train made a welcome departure, were shocking..."

The description "promiscuous promenading" is intriguing; just what gave rise to it and the precise nature of the many complaints is probably tucked away in the archives somewhere so venturing into the realms of speculation here would not be wise – we could jump to all sorts of wrong conclusions! Another point arises: how would such a ban have been

-MAURICE McALEESE-

enforced? It would surely have been difficult. It would be interesting to know also just how long the ban remained in force and if there were any complaints from non-travelling members of the public.

Anyhow, a good description of what it was like to view Portrush for the first time from the window of a railway carriage as the train pulled into the station was given by a travel writer in 1904: "A muddle of grey houses against the sky, a stark rampart of cliff with a string of black rocks at its foot, and about and beyond white foam and tumbling waves, the first impression of Portrush from the windows of a railway train gives the character of the place at a glance…"

During the summer months, Portrush was a magnet for tens of thousands of excursionists in the early part of the last century and nearly all of them arrived by train. For the most part, the outing was pleasant and uneventful, but that was not the case in July, 1913 when the town was terrorised by what the local newspapers described as "a Belfast mob."

They were not bona fide excursionists but had infiltrated a Sunday School party, with the sole purpose, it seemed, of causing mayhem throughout the town. According to one account, their depredations included the removal by force of household goods displayed for sale outside shops in Main Street as well as "…the abstraction of walking sticks and other articles (without payment) from fancy goods stores, and using abusive and threatening language to assistants who interfered."

Several ice-cream carts were overturned and the contents scattered on the street; baskets of strawberries and other fruits were kicked over and other goods belonging to fruit merchants destroyed. The miscreants also raided a stationery shop in the harbour area and stole goods to the value of thirty shillings.

The wrecking spree did not end there: local public houses did not escape. The mob went into several pubs, smashed tumblers and bottles while at the same time removing or damaging pictures and display cases as well as assaulting and chasing individuals who sought to remonstrate with them.

What were the police doing while all this was going on? One news report came up with this answer: "Complaints were, of course, made to the police, but the force, being very small, could not undertake to arrest the offenders through fear of provoking a riot because the rowdies took good care to have a body of sympathisers to support them in the event of interference by the Constabulary."

It would be impossible, the report added, to recount some of the "dastardly acts" for which the rowdies were responsible because elderly persons and ladies, abused and insulted by them, were afraid of worse outrages if they took action to protect themselves and many simply suffered in silence.

The report concluded with a description of what happened in a local restaurant displaying the sign "Please Walk In," an invitation which the band of young hooligans accepted. "After dining sumptuously, they walked out without paying. Not only that, but they carried with them plates, saucers and other articles which they smashed into smithereens in the street."

The town was left reeling after such an orgy of destruction and afterwards the question being asked was: who would pick up the bill for the damage? "It is most likely," speculated one disgruntled trader, "that claims for compensation will be lodged by traders whose goods were removed or their property destroyed – in which case the expense will probably fall upon the innocent ratepayers of the town." One of the news reports concluded with this, rather mild in the circumstances, criticism of the police: "The wonder is that the authorities, having precedents in similar performances, did not materially strengthen the Constabulary force during the present week."

One of these precedents had occurred some weeks earlier and it involved another group of excursionists. All had gone well, apparently, until it was time for them to leave when some of the departing group became rowdy and disorderly, to put it mildly. What made this incident all the more disturbing was the fact that during the fracas, shots were heard to ring out repeatedly along the railway station platform.

One report states: "The scenes at the station, before the train made a welcome departure, were shocking, to say the least of it, shots ringing out along the platform, while it is asserted the cartridges were not of the 'blank' calibre. Of course they were fired in the air, but even so, nothing could be written strong enough to condemn such conduct. People generally go down to 'the Port' for pleasure and it is not enhanced when a rowdy and disorderly crowd proceed to 'paint the town red,' as some so-called excursionists have done recently."

The report concluded with this condemnation: "It is said there is a limit to everything, and one would think it has been about reached in the matter of how rowdies are allowed to annoy the peaceably-inclined, particularly when seeking a holiday."

There is no reference as to how the police handled this disturbance but doubtless they would have been called to the scene, particularly if, as claimed, shots had been fired. And no doubt the local Council would have been concerned also and would have been forthright in its condemnation.

Such conduct was very much the exception rather than the rule and the vast majority of excursions to Portrush were extremely pleasant experiences.

serenading with a scottish twist!

MAURICE MCALEESE

"From early morn until past the hour of midnight, the streets resounded with their merry-making."

S ome interesting insights into the entertainment scene in Portrush in the early years of the last century are contained in a report of the annual meeting of the Portrush Winter Gardens Co. Ltd for the year 1910.

The annual meeting of the shareholders was held in the Station Café and the report lists those present: Messrs J.P.Stott, R. Audinwood, J. Kennedy, M. Keenan, W.W. Hill, W.J. Morrow, W.F. Anderson, S.R. Henry, J.J. McNabb, P. Bradley. F. Kane, N.S. Stewart, P.J. Mains, Miss Hamilton, Miss Woods and the Secretary (Mr. D. MacLaughlin). During the year, a boxball alley and shooting gallery had been provided and a large enclosure for pierrot performances erected at a cost of over £300. The receipts from all these branches had been very satisfactory and the directors hoped for larger returns from the pierrots during the coming year.

With regard to the roller skating rink, thought at the time to be one of the best in the British Isles, it was reported that it was quite evident "that skating had come to stay and the future of it, in Portrush especially, where there was no other attraction, looked bright." The books were in a healthy state, the accounts for the year showing a balance, after writing off depreciation, of £834.12s.6d. and consequently it was proposed to pay a dividend of twelve and a half per cent.

In the same week as the annual meeting, what was described as a musical carnival was held at the skating rink, an event which had attracted the largest attendance so far that particular season. It's worth recording the events making up the programme, if only to show the ingenuity of the organisers.

There were six events, for which prizes were provided, and the winners were as follows: Graceful skating – Miss Dorothy Anderson, Coleraine and Master Horne, Falkirk; balloon race, Mr. David McVicker, Portrush, who also won the variety race; hoop race, Mr. David G. Christie, Coleraine; egg and spoon race, Master Horne, Falkirk; half-mile skating race for amateurs - 1, Mr. David Forde-Hutchinson, Stranocum; 2, Mr. Daniel McVicker, Portrush. The prizes were handed to the winners by Mrs J.P. Stott, Portrush. The judges were Messrs J.P. Stott and Fred Jones (floor manager).

The Winter Gardens Company certainly contributed a great deal to the success and popularity of Portrush as the leading seaside resort in Northern Ireland and just a few years later, in July of 1913, still more improvements were announced. This is taken from a news report: "In its new form and scope, the pavilion of the Portrush Winter Gardens Company was opened on Monday and a very large assemblage of visitors was greatly gratified to note the improvements that have been effected during the past month.

"There are now three handsome and convenient halls within the pavilion, each accommodating about a thousand persons. The stage, which has been fitted up in the variety theatre, is a magnificent one, and the opinion has been generally expressed that it would be hard to find a better one within the province."

Main Street on a busy day.

Within the same complex, there was now also a picture-house and it was claimed that the latest and most up to date pictures were being shown to the delight of a large audience at every session.

A year earlier, a portion of the skating rink had been railed off for dancing so that dancing and skating could now be staged in the rink at the same time, something surely unique to Portrush. "This is certainly a great improvement on the former arrangements," according to another Press report. It went on to give this account of the new arrangement in action: "On Monday evening the floor presented a brilliant and animated spectacle, and the dancing and skating were enjoyed to the fullest extent. The management of the rink, which will be open every night from now until the end of the season, have arranged an attractive programme for the benefit of the large numbers who will doubtless patronise the pavilion."

No expense had been spared, apparently, to ensure that things went with a swing – the Meistersinger's, a well-known band from London, had been hired and their performance on that opening evening was described as "delightful." This had gone down well with "devotees of the terpsichorean art."

The Roller Skating Rink Pavilion, to give it its full title, had been built in 1909 – at a meeting of the Winter Gardens Company in April of that year the tender of a Belfast firm, D. Anderson and Son, was accepted for the construction of the rink on the pleasure grounds adjoining the railway station. The amount of the tender was given as £3,539 and it was expected that the work would be completed at the beginning of July. The building was 250 feet long, 90 feet wide and 25 feet high and a 15 foot wide promenade ran all the way round the rink. Included within the pavilion were a band-stand and six shops as well as accommodation for the provision of light refreshments, cloakrooms and toilets.

The same week the company had placed an advertisement in the local Press seeking tenants for the six shops, specifying the type of business preferred as (1) Tobacco (2) Stationery, Photography and Picture Post Cards (3) Antique and Jewellery (4) Fruits and Flowers (5) Sweets (6) Drapery, Beleek China, Toys and Toilet Requisites.

The tobacco shop would probably have sold a wide selection of cigarettes and pipe tobacco and might even have stocked a few clay pipes. One of the cigarette brands would have been Butterfly cigarettes, described as "light and delicious" and manufactured by a firm called Hignetts. The brand was advertised in the local Press and was promoted as "a cigarette of the highest quality." They were hand made from the finest Virginia tobacco and could be purchased in either packets or by weight – I wonder which was the better value.

There was certainly no lack of entertainment in Portrush in those days as this extract from another old record shows: "A brisk trade has been done in all the places of business and singularly few apartments and houses are unoccupied. Increasing crowds have listened to the military band. 'Uncle Joe' and his party have entertained nightly audiences in front of Lansdowne Terrace. 'The Square' as it is called, has been reserved for the orators, male and female, of the evangelical mission. Attractions of a different kind are offered at the railway recreation grounds. Hanneford's Circus, located at the east side of the town, amused multitudes of visitors and residents on Wednesday and Thursday evenings."

Uncle Joe was a popular entertainer in Portrush, catering for both children and adults for many summers. His performance was mostly outdoors, usually at Craigvara near the Arcadia beach. In July, 1913, one of his shows attracted "such a crowd as had not been seen for many, many moons." The bill was usually an all-star one and Uncle Joe could list among the star performers such names as Harry Lauder, probably the best known, but others such as Tettrazini, Albani, Adeline Genee and Fred Farren.

Harry Lauder would, of course, have had an instant rapport with both children and adults with his unique brand of humour and singing and Fred Farren was a dancer – just what the others included in their acts is not clear but undoubtedly it all went down well. Uncle Joe also liked to involve children in his act – one of his publicity blurbs pointed out: "Not only does the company include many Scottish children, but there are three or four locals, and these amongst his very cleverest pupils."

At his outdoor shows, deck chairs were provided for the audience – he had a supply of 300 – and if lighting was needed on a dull evening, that was not a problem – always on hand was a 500 candle-power lamp!

The summer of 1913 certainly seems to have been particularly successful from the point of view of entertainment. Another report noted: "In no previous year has there been such a galaxy of attractions in Portrush. What with two picture-houses, a variety theatre, a dancing hall, band performances galore, not to speak of the amusements on the East Strand – we include in the latter category Henry Ireland and his donkeys, so popular with the young folks - the town is happily equipped. Then there is a seemingly endless variety of itinerant street musicians, prominent among whom are the little Italian organ-grinders, who do their best to enliven the atmosphere of the main thoroughfare of the township."

Cinema-goers were spoiled for choice – apart from the picture-house in the Pavilion, there was also the Picture Palace in the Town Hall where a new innovation had been introduced – the Vivaphone – and it was proving a great success. This was an instrument devised in the early days of cinema to synchronise sound with motion pictures. It was reported that Mr. Sheridan, the enterprising manager, "is determined that he will not allow interest in the great singing pictures to flag."

For those whose musical taste was a little more refined, there was the tantalising prospect of Madame Levante and her Band, comprising a talented group of young ladies. They were appearing regularly at the Arcadia restaurant and attracting record attendances at concerts featuring Irish and Scottish airs. Madame Levante's choice of music was made "with taste and distinction." Commented one critic: "Only the most valuable and characteristic compositions were contributed, and on each occasion the entertainment was such as to please the most fastidious critic."

At one of Madame Levante's concerts, the guest artiste was Mr. Walter McLelland, a tenor from Belfast, who sang several folk songs and other Irish numbers "in most acceptable fashion." The concerts were held in a large hall of the restaurant and on another occasion, when the programme was exclusively Scottish, it was crowded to an almost uncomfortable extent. The performance, it was said, generally enhanced the already enviable reputation which Madame Levante's company had gained in Portrush.

One announcement of the arrival of Madame Levante and her band indicated that they would be giving indoor and alfresco performances daily.

It concluded: "Residents remember with pleasure the treat of the season which Madame Levante and her clever ladies gave in the Town Hall last winter."

Band promenades, or concerts, were a popular means of entertainment in Portrush – the Urban Council even had a Band Committee to procure the services of top bands for the summer programme. But in the summer of 1904 there was obviously some

Eglinton Crescent, Portrush

37

difficulty in this regard because it was noted in the Press: "Band promenades are still lacking in Portrush, notwithstanding the effort that was made by the Urban Council to procure a first-class combination for the summer."

It was not only organised entertainment: sometimes the visitors provided their own version of street entertainment, particularly the Scottish visitors. "From early morn until well past the midnight hour, the streets resound with their merry-making," according to one observer. "Good natured and the jolliest of people they are. We welcome them and extend to them each recurring year a genuine 'caed mile failthe' and delight in seeing them thoroughly enjoying themselves…"

It seems the Scottish visitors had a penchant for sing-songs "especially during the fleeting moments before the advent of another day." It was a form of serenading that was not always appreciated: "When a number of them gather underneath the ordinary native's bedroom window and display their vocal qualities to concertina or other instrumental accompaniment, he may be tempted to say or do things which are better left unsaid or undone." At such times the otherwise attractive tunes such as "Dixieland" or "Cowboy Joe" or the ever popular "Annie Laurie" sounded positively irritating and annoying.

It did not, apparently, result in anyone being drenched with water thrown from a bedroom window, or hit by a flower-pot, at least no such incident has been recorded!

- MAURICE McALEESE -

hazel's
first run

*"She was an impressive looking ship
of fine appearance and graceful lines."*

When the s.s. "Hazel" made her initial run from Ardrossan to Portrush on the morning of Thursday, June 13, 1907, the only passengers on board were the directors of the Laird Line and selected guests. The weather was dull and threatening as the sparkling new flag-bedecked vessel slipped her moorings at Montgomerie Pier and slowly steamed towards the open sea.

The well-heralded trip to Portrush would take just over four hours and this in spite of the adverse weather conditions - a strong head-wind prevailed that day and the running tide was against the steamer all the way to Rathlin Island. In spite of this, the Hazel made good time, skirting close to the coastline on the run-in to Portrush – crowds thronged the headlands at Fair Head and Ballycastle and gave her a rousing welcome as she passed. In return, Captain Hately replied with the traditional nautical salute – a loud blast on the steamer's foghorn.

A reporter on board the vessel wrote: "Although the sea was rather heavy between Fair Head and Ramore, the Hazel behaved admirably, and the passengers experienced no inconvenience except from the rain which at times caused their withdrawal from the bracing breezes of the North Atlantic."

By now, the steamer was within sight of Portrush where a huge crowd of spectators awaited her arrival. They crammed onto the main vantage point, Ramore Head, and although it was raining their excitement and enthusiasm were not diminished. The Hazel's "jaunty display of flags" was answered in similar fashion from the Coastguard lookout and as she steamed closer still there was a scramble over the grassy slopes to find better vantage points as she rounded the headland.

LAIRD LINE, LTD

SEASON ·1908·

TOURS IN IRELAND

LAIRD LINE, LTD
52, Robertson St,
GLASGOW.

This is how the last stage of the historic voyage was described in one report: "The run towards Blackrock for the turn into the harbour was promptly accomplished, and a few moments later the Hazel, under Captain Hately's unerring guidance, entered between the pier ends amid hearty cheers from the crowd assembled on the wharf, the trip having been accomplished within four and a half hours, indicating that on a fine day the steamer will be able to do the run well inside that time."

To celebrate the event, a sumptuous lunch prepared by the Hazel's catering staff was served on board the vessel - the special guests included representatives of the Urban Council, Portrush Harbour Company and Coleraine Harbour Board.

The menu was mouth-watering and for the record, this was the choice: Soup – Hotch Potch; boiled salmon; Dutch sauce; fillets of sole; Tartare sauce. Entrees – Chicken cutlets; tomato sauce; prawns; Joints – Roast sirloin of beef; roast lamb; mint sauce; roast turkey. Sweet – Swiss tart; green gooseberry tart; orange creams; "Hazel" pudding; jellies; custard; meringues. Salad, Cheese, Ices, Tea, Coffee etc.

A series of toasts followed the lunch and there was much praise for the Laird Shipping Line for having commissioned such a magnificent vessel for the Portrush-Ardrossan run. The harbour at Portrush had been dredged a couple of months earlier to ensure enough depth of water and the Harbour Company were praised for their efforts in this regard. The work had been carried out with the help and advice of the Hazel's skipper, Captain E. R. Hately and he was also praised for his expertise in bringing the vessel so skilfully alongside the dock.

That was no mean feat because the harbour had been designed to accommodate vessels of about 100 feet in length – the Hazel measured 268 feet and had a draught of just over 23 feet. On trials prior to the inaugural run she had achieved a speed of 19 knots.

For her day, she was an impressive looking ship "of fine appearance and graceful lines" and she had been fitted out to a high degree of excellence for the comfort of passengers. There were four decks consisting of the lower, main bridge, and two boat decks. First-class passengers had the exclusive use of the bridge deck amidships. The level of comfort was said to be up to hotel standards and there was a tea room "neatly finished in light oak, with tulip wood inlay panels" which would be run "on city lines."

The boat deck was no less impressive; it boasted a large smoke room, finished in oak, with red marble tables. There was also a handsome deck lounge finished in luxurious upholstery, and private state rooms for first class passengers. Second-class passengers were not too badly catered for either – they had a large dining saloon on the main deck, fitted out "in a neat style" and there was an adjoining bar.

On the poop deck was another saloon, described as large and airy for the exclusive use of second-class lady passengers. It also had toilet facilities. The main mid-ship deck, for its entire length, could be utilised as a promenade for second-class passengers and in wet weather it could be used as a shelter.

The Hazel was a ship to be proud of and the Laird Line stressed: "In the general arrangements the comfort of the passengers has been made the first consideration; but not the least striking feature of the new boat is the speed, and it is estimated that she will cover the distance between Ardrossan and the popular North of Ireland seaside resort of Portrush, in about four hours. The vessel is also fitted with two bilge keels to minimise the rolling."

The arrangements were that the Hazel would sail every weekday from Ardrossan at 9.45am in connection with trains from Dundee, Perth, Stirling, Edinburgh and Glasgow and with principle stations in Lanarkshire, Dumbartonshire, Renfrewshire and Ayrshire. It was due to arrive in Portrush at 1.35pm and this, it was felt, would enable ongoing passengers to reach surrounding towns like Coleraine, Ballymoney, Ballycastle, Ballymena, Cookstown, Limavady and Londonderry in a reasonable time.

On the return journey the Hazel would leave Portrush at 3.30pm, reaching Ardrossan at 8.30pm, Glasgow at 9.40 and ongoing passengers to Edinburgh about 11pm.

The Hazel had her trial cruise a week earlier with 250 invited guests on board when the route was from Gourock around the Isle of Arran. And according to one account, it was a memorable outing: "From a wet, depressing early morning a slight improvement suggested itself during the rail run from Glasgow to Gourock; and although the start was made under circumstances none too bright, there was in the temperature the promise of better things in the afternoon. The steamers powers were put to a fair test, and all on board were convinced, before the Cumbraes had been passed, that she would do credit to designers, builders and owners in the task for which she has been specially constructed."

On that trial voyage, the Hazel ran into choppy waters after rounding Arran and Pladda but so well was she built that passengers experienced only the slightest "roll" and only a couple of inexperienced passengers were sea sick. On the return trip to Gourock she called at Wemyss Bay pier to land a few passengers. The trial run lasted six hours during which a mean speed of 19 knots was maintained and the general opinion was that the new steamer had more than realised the expectations of owners and passengers alike. It was back in the summer of 1902 that the Laird Line decided that its steamship service to Portrush should run from Ardrossan and not, as hitherto, from Gourock, the main reason being that this would reduce the sea passage to just over four hours. A report in one of the Glasgow papers noted that the change would not be so convenient for people in the Greenock and Port-Glasgow areas but to compensate for this very cheap through fares from these towns to Ardrossan had been arranged. The price of a steerage return, it was pointed out, would be only sixpence more than from Paisley, where the return to Portrush was eight shillings.

It had been towards the end of the previous century that the Laird Line had introduced a daylight passenger steamship service between Gorouck and Portrush and the undertaking proved very successful. The main ship on that old route was the Azalea. It was "a commodious steamer" and was a familiar sight on the northern coastline for a good few years, operating a daily service. In the summer of 1900, the Laird Line announced that another steamer, the Cedar, a sister ship to the Azalea, was also to be put on the route. A newspaper commented: "We hope that this magnificent service will reap its due reward, and convince the company that the public nowadays are not slow to appreciate any efforts made by them to successfully cater for their requirements."

The steamship passenger service between Portrush and Ardrossan ceased on the outbreak of the Great War and it was not resumed afterwards. The Hazel was eventually sold to the Isle of Man Steam Packet Company to replace ships lost in the war. For some unexplained reason she was later renamed "Mona" and for many years carried passengers and cargo to and from the Isle of Man. She was only ever involved in one serious incident and that was in July, 1930 when she ran aground on Conister Rock – at high tide she was re-floated with the aid of tugs and was only slightly damaged. In 1938 she was withdrawn from service and sold for scrap, a sad ending for a once proud old lady of the sea who had played a very important role in contributing to that golden age of seaside holidays in Portrush.

a Link with the world's first film star

A t the beginning of the twentieth century, motion pictures were a big attraction in Portrush and a popular entertainment for holidaymakers. In the days when the resort did not have a purpose-built cinema, films were shown at two locations - the Town Hall and the Pavilion - and they were very well supported.

I've discovered that Portrush has a link with a long forgotten star of the silent silver screen going back almost to the very beginning of the motion picture industry. John Bunny was an important star before Charlie Chaplin came on the scene - some sources say he was the world's first film star. He was certainly the first comedy star of the American silver screen, having starred in a whole series of "John Bunny" films.

Back in the summer of 1913, he was in Portrush where he was seen "strolling unassumingly" along the seafront and he would certainly have stood out from the crowd. He was a big man, weighing 300 pounds and his figure was described as "rotund." One reference says he exploited his weight and shape to his advantage in many of his film plots.

That summer the Picture Palace cinema in Portrush – it was in the Town Hall - was showing a film of the Charles Dickens classic, "The Pickwick Papers" in which John Bunny had the starring role. Apparently it was one of the few excursions he made into dramatic acting and although he acquitted himself well, it was for his comic talents that he was best known.

He was only 52 when he died at his home in Brooklyn, just a couple of years after he took that unassuming stroll along the seafront in Portrush. So his film career was relatively short and that may account for the fact that, unlike Chaplain, he is not remembered today. The only reference I can find to his

Portrush visit is in a Press release in connection with the showing of The Pickwick Papers at the Picture Palace. In a commentary on the film, it states: "…the character of Mr. Pickwick is portrayed with masterly conception by John Bunny, a cinema actor who perhaps has obtained a greater vogue and enjoys a larger retinue of admirers of humorous characters than any other actor yet screened. It will be interesting to many to know that John Bunny was to be seen a short time ago in the flesh strolling unassumingly along the front at Portrush."

Not too many people, it seems, knew that a film star of his stature was in town so it may have been a private visit. At any rate, it's a nice little piece of Portrush cinematic history which, incidentally, did not get its first properly designed cinema until a year after Bunny's visit when The Picture House in Main Street opened its doors to the public in July, 1914. It was "a highly auspicious opening" and the new cinema was under the experienced management of Mr. R.L. Sheridan.

Here is a description of the Picture House, taken from one of the news reports of the opening: "A wide and brightly-lighted entrance hall leads from the street to the new house of entertainment, which is most comfortably seated and otherwise attractive, and the ventilation is perfect.

"The deeply sloping floor is a novel feature in Portrush and enables ladies to wear their hats without feeling that they may be obstructing the view of those who are sitting behind them. Every requisite to a cinema house has been supplied, and by means of its emergency doors and wide entrance, the hall can be quickly emptied.

"On the opening night the house was crowded, and for brilliance and steadiness the pictures could not be excelled. That the house is found to be a most attractive place of entertainment is shown by the large audiences which are nightly patronising it. On Monday and Tuesday next week "The Lure of Gold" will be shown, on Wednesday and Thursday "For the Freedom of Cuba" and on Friday and Saturday "The Soul of the Sea."

The report concluded with the teaser that Mr. Sheridan, it was understood, had procured some of the most exclusive films on the market for showing in August and September.

The new Picture House got off to a really good start by the sound of things and it signalled the end of the Picture Palace in the Town Hall. It had been very well supported for a few years and this extract from an earlier news item is fairly typical: "The Picture Palace at the Town Hall continues to attract large audiences and last week, when the strangely fascinating and impressive "Quo Vadis" was unrolled, scores of persons had to be refused admission twice daily."

Its popularity was not only due to the films shown, as highlighted in another report: "The Picture Palace has been a centre of much attraction this week, a number of exceptionally good films being exhibited. On Wednesday and Thursday evenings Mr. Percy French, the well-known entertainer, gave excellent performances at intervals and, in common with the pictures, these were immensely enjoyed. Mr. French is an old favourite in Portrush, as elsewhere, and his return visit this week was greatly appreciated."

The opening of The Picture House also signalled the end of films being shown in The Pavilion, which must have been a spacious building because it had room not only for a picture-house but also a dancing hall, skating rink and a variety theatre.

Apart from the usual bill of fare, sometimes the Pavilion screened what was termed "a topical picture" and this was often a film made of holiday activities in the town. This was also the case in the Picture Palace. For instance, at the opening of the season in the summer of 1913, a film of Coleraine Regatta was shown. It had been filmed by the manager, Mr.

Sheridan, and some of the close finishes he managed to capture on film evoked rounds of applause from the audience, demonstrating his "cleverness and versatility." Not too many cinema managers, even in those days, would have had the thrill of being able to screen films they had made themselves.

Mrs Sheridan was not left out of the picture. During intervals in the programme her pianoforte contributions greatly contributed to the enjoyment. So the couple were a formidable combination.

The films were mostly shown by an organisation calling itself the Irish Living Picture Company. At

Phyllis Dare
A famous
actress
of her day

the beginning of the season in 1913 they claimed to have "a magnificent programme" and were confident in predicting as prosperous a run as they had enjoyed the previous year.

This is an extract from their Press release: "For Monday and Tuesday a great and exciting drama called 'High Treason' will be screened but the greatest attraction is undoubtedly the star for Wednesday and Thursday, the Phyllis Dare and George Grossmith film. This is an exclusive, the company having obtained sole permission to exhibit this in Portrush. The two universal favourites to be shown to the cinema public for the first time need no introduction. We can only advise all to secure their places to witness this great attraction beforehand, as the anticipated crowded houses will, without doubt, be realised."

The programme for Friday and Saturday was a showing of Charles Dickens classic "The Pickwick Papers", with the lead role being played by John Bunny, as mentioned earlier. The intriguing question remains: what was a star of his magnitude doing in Portrush that summer of 1913? Perhaps it was simply a private visit. It seems unlikely that he would have been shooting scenes for a film because that would have attracted a good deal of attention and it would have been hard to avoid publicity.

Perhaps, on that little Portrush stroll of his, he would have stopped to have a look at one of the minstrel shows – as a young man, he had joined a small minstrel show and had toured the east coast of America with the company. In an interview for Motion Picture Magazine in 1913, the year of his Portrush visit, he said: "I believe the time is coming when motion picture machines will be a part of the equipment of every school and college in the country, and many branches of learning now so objectionable to children will be made interesting by the use of motion pictures. My principal worry is that I can't hope to live long enough to do all the work that I've mapped out for myself." His words were prophetic. He died in Brooklyn, New York on April 26, 1915. He well deserved the honour he was eventually given of a star on Vine Street's Walk of Fame memorial in Hollywood.

The intriguing questions surrounding John Bunny's visit to Portrush in those early days of the motion picture industry will probably remain unanswered.

"He was seen 'strolling unassumingly' along the seafront."

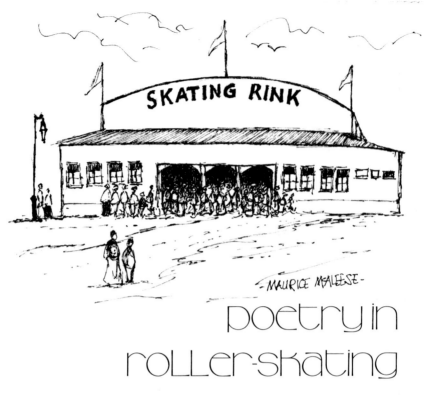

- MAURICE M^cALEESE -

poetry in roller-skating motion

Where there's a wheel I'll find a way
To go rinking – rinking – rinking.

One of the most significant developments in Portrush, from a tourism point of view at the beginning of the last century was the opening of a state of the art roller-skating rink right in the centre of the town. It was a huge attraction and gave a tremendous boost to the resort's appeal as a holiday destination.

The whole concept behind the building was very clever – it had been designed and constructed in such a way that should the craze for roller-skating diminish, it could be easily converted and adapted for other purposes.

It was located on a site adjacent to the railway station and was provided by the Winter Gardens Company. Of timber construction, it was 256 feet long, 92 feet wide and 35 feet high. The floor area for skating was 210 feet by 60 feet and was the most important feature of the building, of course. The skating surface was of rock maple wood laid down over a surface of spruce and this was by far the most laborious part of the work – the inch thick maple was comprised of two and a quarter inch wide strips, tongued and grooved so they could be slotted together.

This description is taken from an old brochure: "Round the whole circumference of the skating floor runs a promenade 15 feet wide, and separated from the main floor by a railing upholstered in American leather. On the side next the sea, in the centre of the space, is the band-stand, and at either side are three rows of seats arranged in tiers one above the other, leaving a space six feet wide for the promenade. A large space at the upper end of the promenade on this side is reserved for refreshments, which will be supplied under the management of the Midland Railway Company, and it is the intention that afternoon teas shall form a special feature of the catering.

Pleasure Grounds, Portrush.

"The public will enter the Rink through a patent self-registering turnstile, placed in the centre of a covered space 24 feet by 8 feet. At each side of the entrance is a series of rooms which will be fitted up as offices, skate and cloak rooms, lavatories etc. In addition to one exit door for general use, there will be five large emergency doors with patent fittings so that they will fly open when subjected to a certain pressure. Six small shops are being erected at various points around the building, at the lower or west end of which is another series of rooms, including the kitchen, a dynamo and engine room."

The plans for lighting the building were no less impressive, the dynamo, driven by a 24 horse-power gas engine, being used for generating the electricity as required. This supplied the power needed to light the front of the building with two powerful electric lamps and the interior by twelve flame arc lamps each of 3,000 candle power. As the brochure pointed out: "Thus brilliantly illuminated, a beautiful effect will be imparted to the spacious interior by the addition of two hundred small incandescent electric lamps fitted as Japanese lanterns."

The directors of the Winter Gardens Company certainly had put a lot of thought into the building because they insisted that the design should take into account its exposed situation close to the seafront "necessitating strength and rigidity" and, interestingly, the probable falling away of roller-skating as a pastime and the future adaptation of the building for the holding of concerts, theatrical performances and other entertainments and amusements.

The weather had not been all that good for most of the month of July that summer so the newly opened Skating Rink was a welcome refuge and it was reported in the local Press that some remarkably fine skating was witnessed "though American and English performers have vied not unsuccessfully with their compeers of Ireland and Scotland in the gracefulness of this new locomotion on four tiny wheels."

The proprietors had taken the precaution of imposing a speed limit on the rink to curb any racers but even going at a fairly fast pace, it still took about forty seconds to do a full circle of the rink. Someone was inspired to write a poem about the new facility:

> On causeway cool at ease I flit
> Upon my rollers resting;
> In merry mood, if e'er I fall,
> I smile – and rise up jesting.
> The gay attendant fits my skates,
> My arm I soon am linking
> In Angeline's, and off we fly
> A rinking – rinking – rinking.

> To stand in equilibrium
> At first was quite a plague;
> I often to a Nether Land,
> Whose chief town's not the Hague,
> Consigned the whole establishment
> (The fact will bear no blinking),
> Together with the man who first
> Tried rinking – rinking – rinking.

But now I find the more I rink,
The more I want to skate;
The sole ambition of my life
Is to increase my rate.
There's nothing like an evening roll,
With plenty of high-jinking;
Where there's a wheel I'll find a way –
To go rinking – rinking – rinking.

How's that for a little bit of poetry in motion! As might be expected, there was an enormous attendance at the opening of the new Skating Rink which, amazingly, had been erected in the space of just eight weeks. It was very well covered in the local Press. This from one of the reports: "Long before the skating began, the whole of the seats in the promenade were occupied, and the skating floor was bordered by rows of interested spectators. By and by the band – Beattie's band from Glasgow, which has been engaged for the season – struck up a merry tune, and a score of skaters glided over the ample floor, led by the uniformed instructors employed by the Company. The number of skaters of both sexes rapidly increased, until at one time there was almost 400 on the floor."

Another report noted: "Many of the more skilful performers were extremely elegant, now waltzing round, now gliding past on one leg, then moving rapidly backwards, and again skimming away in most graceful evolutions. Truly the poetry of motion, and the most witching pastime of the day!"

Just watching the skaters in action had its own entertainment value and the accompanying music was worth listening to, adding to the "bewildering charm in the endless stream of skaters, with an occasional fall to enliven the scene."

Even when the band stopped playing for occasional breaks, the noise of the many skaters was "by no means unpleasant" and the sound, according to one scribe, "falls upon the ear like the constant roll of a heavy sea on the shore."

It was the beginning of a new era of entertainment in Portrush.

a Little bit of bathing history

"…the first resort in the United Kingdom to adopt mixed bathing. And a very sensible suggestion too."
-Nomad's Weekly.

The summer of 1901 marked a milestone in the history of bathing in Portrush. That summer, for the first time, "mixed" bathing was permitted and it was claimed in some quarters that Portrush was the first seaside resort in the United Kingdom to remove the usually strictly enforced gender segregation rule for bathers.

The decision to relax the bye-laws to allow this to happen, was taken at a meeting of the Town Council and it meant that for the first time, mixed bathing was permitted at the South Pier at the harbour and at the Blue Pool, two of the most popular bathing places hitherto reserved for male bathers.

When the first ladies took the plunge at these two favourite spots, they were making a really big splash in bathing history but there does not seem to have been an official ceremony of any kind and the event is not recorded in any of the source material I have been able to consult.

Notices were to be erected at both the Blue Pool and the harbour indicating that "bathing is only permitted on the conditions dictated by law and decency." Presumably there would also have been a notice interpreting in some more specific way the term "law and decency."

There were no restrictions imposed on the ladies bathing from the South Pier – they could bathe there at any time they wished – but that was not the case at the Blue Pool where they were only allowed to bathe at certain reserved times in the mornings and afternoons. Why it was felt necessary to make this distinction is not clear, but it must not have worked out satisfactorily because the Council later changed its bye-laws yet again and the ban on the ladies bathing at the Blue Pool, was re-imposed.

Portrush was credited with becoming the first seaside resort in the United Kingdom to permit mixed bathing in an article which appeared in "Nomad's Weekly," a satirical magazine published in Belfast with a circulation of 40,000.

At the South Pier
- a nice dive.

"The first town in the United Kingdom," it was noted, "to utilise electric traction, (a reference to the Giant's Causeway tramway) now the Urban Council have, by their recent bye-law permitting ladies to bathe at the South Pier and Blue Pool, made Portrush the first resort in the United Kingdom to adopt mixed bathing. And a very sensible suggestion too, those who know anything will say.

"If it will do anything, as it certainly will, to shame the males, whose hypothetical bathing garment is more often than not the triangular clout which passes for decency, mixed bathing will become a blessing at Portrush."

A Coleraine lady later wrote to the Council seeking clarification on behalf of a large number of young ladies who were learning to swim. She wanted to know if the swimming master had leave to attend with his ropes and belts to give the usual lessons. The Council replied by sending her a copy of the bye-law.

Just why the ban on ladies at the Blue Pool was re-imposed isn't too clear but later that summer there were complaints about the behaviour of young men during the times when it was reserved for the ladies. They would congregate around the rocks and the ladies must have felt intimidated by their presence, that the privacy which they were now entitled to was being invaded. Perhaps it had something to do with that and the only way the Council felt able to control the situation was to re-introduce the ban on the ladies which doesn't seem all that fair. Be that as it may, for a good many years afterwards, the Blue Pool continued as a men only bathing place. It remained, however, a contentious issue with the ladies and, ironically, they resorted to the same tactics as those young men they had complained about:

"There is still a good deal of grumbling about ladies congregating in the vicinity of the pool and squatting there for hours at a time. Bathers and the attendant alike would feel grateful if our fair friends would find a resting-place elsewhere…"

Quite large numbers of ladies had been congregating on the natural amphitheatre of rocks overlooking the pool. It was not a conventional pool but a rocky sea inlet in the shape of a horse-shoe. There were high and low diving boards and a splendid water chute. At regular intervals during the summer it was the venue for spectacular diving displays, an important part of the holiday entertainment programme. During that particular summer, because of the exceptionally fine weather, the Blue Pool and other bathing spots had been very busy.

Perhaps the ladies on the rocks were making some kind of unspoken protest, their very presence indicating that they were not at all happy that they were being excluded from this sheltered and very well equipped location.

They were causing waves and in the local Press they were getting a fair bit of stick. Even some visitors to Portrush were making their feelings known. This is what one of them wrote: "If those ladies who are in the habit of congregating on the rocks at the Blue Pool would kindly direct their attention to some of the entertainments which are so plentiful, bathers frequenting this place would feel gratified.

Bathing at Murtagh's Mouth

"As many as thirty men and boys have been anxious to get in for a bathe but with a crowd of females in the vicinity they declined to enter the water and have threatened to stop going there. On Sunday there were almost 300 ladies seated near the bathing-boxes, and large numbers of young fellows who wended their way thither for a bathe, had to go away disappointed. This is scarcely fair to the attendant, who has to depend on the bathers' fees for his profit after defraying his rent for the pool.

"Sometimes even ladies from the neighbouring bathing place make excursions over to the Blue Pool and use the water chute. Seeing mixed bathing is not allowed at this place, the Urban Council should take steps to have a certain area kept free from encroachment."

So it seems that some ladies were quite brazen about the whole thing, ignoring the ban, succumbing to the lure of the long water chute and making a splash in more ways than one no doubt!

In fact, the matter was raised at a meeting of the town Council. A newspaper report of the subsequent debate appeared under the headline: Bathing at the Blue Pool – Presence of Ladies. The debate centred once more as to whether or not the Council should lift the ban and allow mixed bathing at the Blue Pool.

It seems that the pool attendant was on the side of the ladies. Although he was not present at the meeting, he had the support of some of the councillors and they made the point that they should either allow mixed bathing or else prevent the ladies from going there at all. It was claimed that because of the ladies, who gathered there in very large numbers, especially on Sundays, very little bathing was being done at the pool and the attendant was therefore suffering financially.

The ladies found an advocate in the Council chairman who said they simply went to witness the Sunday "exhibition". He felt that if the gentlemen didn't bathe at that time the ladies wouldn't go there.

In the view of some councillors it was a Catch 22 situation – many of the gentlemen stayed away, it was claimed, because of the presence of ladies. Others countered that the ladies went to see the expert divers, adding that " the non-divers are laughed at."

At this point, the Clerk of the Council interjected to explain that they could not allow mixed bathing at the Blue Pool for this season at any rate because they had let the Harbour on the basis that it was the only mixed bathing place in town.

Still, some councillors were not happy, one pointing out that he could not see the sense of allowing mixed bathing at one place and prohibiting it at another. Presumably he had not been at the meeting when the various bathing strategies and concessions were being decided.

From the same councillor came a dire warning that if something was not done to remedy the state of affairs, the Blue Pool might have to be closed altogether because financially it was "not worth looking after." He was supported by a colleague who claimed the Council had no powers to keep the ladies away if they wished to go there. The place belonged, he said, to Lord Antrim, and any lady who wished to bathe there could do so independent of the Council.

When two other councillors attempted to table a motion in favour of allowing the ladies to bathe at the pool, the Clerk again interjected – this would be illegal, he explained.

Still, some councillors were not convinced and remained adamant that if it added to the enjoyment of the visiting public to allow mixed bathing, they did not see why it should be opposed by the Council.

The only lady member of the Council had kept silent until this point. She took exception to some of the remarks made about the ladies, both inside and outside the Council chamber, adding that it was "very ungrateful to speak of the ladies in the way they had been spoken of."

"What," she asked, "would the attendants do on the day of a display if they had not the ladies to go round with the collection boxes?"

That did not cut any ice with one of her male colleagues who said he knew gentlemen who had bathed at the pool for twenty years and they would not go there now because of the presence of ladies. That prompted this retort from a councillor who may have been trying to make some kind of social comment: "Twenty years ago," he said, "ladies wouldn't have gone there to watch gentlemen bathing."

The decision of the Council following that debate is one which may or may not have helped to resolve the issue, at least for that particular season: "Ultimately, it was agreed to have notices posted up stating that the attendant complained of the presence of ladies at the Pool, except at displays, as it was affecting him financially."

At a meeting of the Council some years earlier, in the summer of 1902, the bathing dilemma was given a new twist – this time it was the lady bathers complaining about men. At the meeting, the Clerk said a number of ladies had complained about gentlemen congregating at their bathing-place. After some debate, the Clerk was instructed to issue notices cautioning gentlemen against this practice.

It was not until the summer of 1916 that the question of mixed bathing at the Blue Pool was finally resolved when the Council decided by the narrowest of margins – just one vote – that ladies should be permitted to bathe there as well as the men. One of the councillors highlighted the fact that Portrush was a public resort "and the man who was afraid to bathe in the open sea need not be there at all." What, he asked, was the difference between seeing a woman in a bathing costume at the Blue Pool and watching one on the screen at the cinema?

The Council had been under some pressure to lift the ban on the ladies – a number of petitions had been sent to the council by regular visitors to Portrush, mostly from Belfast, who enjoyed bathing at the Blue Pool, which was described in one of the petitions as the most popular bathing centre in the north of Ireland. The view was also expressed that mixed bathing was now in vogue "in all maritime parts of the kingdom."

It marked the end of a long and difficult chapter in the history of bathing at this popular venue.

754/274   The Harbour, Portrush.

when the
circus
came to
town

*"It's nice to think that Portrush has this link
with a fascinating piece of circus history."*

O ne of the most thrilling and exciting spectacles on the streets of
Portrush in those early summers of the twentieth century must
surely have been when the circus came to town. The parade through
the town was itself a huge attraction and a good way of drumming up
business for the big tent performances.

One of the best of the circuses to come to Portrush in those days was the
Hanneford Circus and like most of the others, it was family owned. Almost
a century has elapsed since its last performance in Ireland, but in spite of
many problems along the way, it is still going strong and today its centre of
operations is in America.

The circus site in Portrush was usually in a field at Cloughorr, just off the
Bushmills Road, where afternoon and evening performances were given
each day. Mostly the visits were for about a week or so at a time.

In July 1910 the Hanneford Circus rolled into town and was given an ecstatic
welcome by residents and holidaymakers. They lined the streets to greet
the amazing array of wagons, animals and performers which made up the
colourful and noisy cavalcade. It consisted of thirty brightly painted wagons
pulled by 100 horses. Included was a small menagerie of camels, an
elephant and ten lions, two wolves, two hyenas, a bear and a tiger. In those
days there were no rumblings about wild animals being used in circuses,

indeed they were seen as a vital part of the appeal and generally speaking the animals were well treated.

The Hanneford circus also had 25 performing horses and of course Portrush was just one of the many towns and hamlets throughout Ireland where it performed.

The husband and wife owners, Ned and Elizabeth Hanneford, both came from circus families and not only did they run the circus but they were also among the star performers. Ned put on a very exciting knife throwing act and his wife, an accomplished tight-rope walker, provided plenty of thrills on the high wire. She also had a daring horse-riding act - one of her specialities involved the use of white doves which were trained to fly to her while she was on horseback performing a series of figure eights in the sawdust ring.

The Hannefords had brought their circus to Ireland in 1903 and for the next nine years they toured the length and breadth of the country, making a name for themselves as a top class travelling circus. It is said to have grown and prospered while in Ireland, both in size and quality.

It is not known how often the Hanneford Circus would have come to Portrush in the course of those nine years but because it was undoubtedly the main seaside resort in Northern Ireland, catering for large numbers of tourists each summer, it's fairly safe to say that it would have appeared at some stage every summer. The link with Ireland was broken when, in 1912, for a variety of reasons, the family decided to start touring in England and Scotland.

The Hanneford Family Circus has been based in America since the late 1920s and is still a big name there to this day. Interestingly, the present-day owners would like to hear from anyone who might have any old photographs of the circus during its time in Portrush or indeed any other venue in Ireland, from 1903 to 1911. The circus website contains this appeal: "If you know anything about this, or can give us details where we can find any information…or indeed, have any pictures of the Hanneford show from that period, we are very interested in obtaining copies of those pictures, or anything else that's pertinent to our family."

Perhaps there is, in some long lost album in an attic somewhere, photographs or posters of that famous old circus in Portrush. And of course, that "perhaps" need not be confined to Portrush because the vast majority of the audiences would have been made up of holidaymakers from all over the place. So let's hope that some photographic evidence does exist and that it comes to light. It's nice to think that Portrush has this link to a fascinating little piece of circus history.

Another circus which called at Portrush at that time was the Circus Ginnett, then one of the UK's largest circuses. It was established in the early 1800s, making it one of the oldest circus families in Europe. At the outbreak of the 1914-18 war, the War Office confiscated the 200 or so horses owned by Ginnett for the war effort and because of this the circus closed down for a period. But after a few twists and turns over the years, it is still going today thanks to succeeding generations of the family keeping the tradition alive.

The Lloyd's Mexican Circus also had Portrush on its touring programme at the turn of the century. One of its headline acts featured a football match with a difference – it was played on bicycles! It must have been hugely entertaining to watch.

One of the stars of this circus was a man from County Clare who became quite famous as "The Singing Clown" not only in Ireland but also in America where he toured with other circuses. John Patterson was the gifted composer of such songs as "Off to Philadelphia in the Morning," "The Stone Outside Dan Murphy's Door" and "The Garden where the Praties Grow". He died tragically when he was just 49. He was singing his own song, "Do Your Best for One Another," which urged loyalist and nationalists to set aside their differences when he was attacked and died in hospital three days later from his injuries.

His memory is immortalised in a painting by Jack B. Yeats entitled, "The Singing Clown" which is said to be a poignant recreation of a figure from Yeats' youth.

bad day at salmon rock

– MAURICE McALEESE –

*"They flutter for a while in the gay vortex
of brief seaside existence, and vanish like
butterflies at season's close."*

Quite a lot of attention was given to the health and safety of bathers in the early days of the last century when Portrush was recognised as the premier bathing resort not only on the north coast, but probably in the whole of Ireland.

The writer of a travel article published in "The Lady of the House", a Dublin magazine, was not thinking only of bathing when he wrote: "Irish folk who take pleasure in spending their annual holidays in Tramore, Youghal, Kilkee, Salthill, Bundoran, Bray, Greystones, Buncrana, etc., should note Portrush as fully equal in attractions to any of the places mentioned, and may accept my assurance that they will not be disappointed by finding their experience less agreeable than elsewhere in Ireland."

In May, 1904, a local reporter observed: "Few places can surpass Portrush as regards sea bathing, and the glories of the Blue Pool are known far and wide. The ladies also are well looked after and, now that mixed bathing is becoming more popular, the Council have provided a number of bathing boxes for ladies at the South Pier."

"Too often at the seaside," it was noted in another Press report, "the sea is the thing that matters least; music, costumes and amusements are the real attractions, and the glories of wave and shore are valued only as a decorative background for the pleasant comedy. In Portrush, this is reversed; here they usurp the whole of the stage, and those who are not satisfied that this should be so would be well advised to spend their holidays elsewhere."

So what was "the pleasant comedy" like among the bathing fraternity in Portrush in those far-off summers? An amusing description by "Clio" in a piece entitled "Seaside Life" published in the *"Constitution"* refers to "... the amphibious young men who in the morning come from the Blue Pool with rolls of towels around their necks, and spend the day consuming cigarettes in the company of other boys' sisters. You know every one of them by sight or by name. They flutter for a while in the gay vortex of brief seaside existence, and vanish like butterflies at summer's close."

In the same year, it seems that bathing had never been so widely indulged in at Portrush. One reason advanced for this was because the Urban Council had "wisely improved the unequalled bathing facilities which Nature has provided and put competent men in charge of the different places. The health-improving pastime has become more popular than ever it was, and as safety can always be assured at any stage of the tide, some of the bathing-places are always certain to be fully occupied. Mixed bathing is becoming more general than heretofore."

> The health-improving pastime has become more popular than ever it was...

Bathing was frequently high on the agenda of the Urban Council and it must be said they were at pains to ensure that the best possible facilities were provided at the various locations.

An old notice published by the Council from June, 1903 sets out a number of "Hints for Visitors" and this is the information given relating to bathing:

Bathing (Gentlemen only) – Blue Pool; attendant, Charles McAllister. (Ladies) – Murtagh's Mouth; attendant, John Hopkins. (Mixed) – South Pier; attendant, James McAllister. (Children) – Rock Ryan; attendant, Mrs Adams. Swimming lessons given at each place by the attendant.

The bathing-place at Murtagh's Mouth, not too far from the more romantically named Blue Pool, was reserved for ladies who enjoyed deep water swimming and diving but it was not so well appointed. So in June, 1904 the Council was considering improving the amenities at Murtagh's Mouth which, like the Blue Pool, was formed by a natural inlet washed by the open sea. According to a Press report of the Council meeting, the improvements entailed providing another bathing-place at this location and the cost of making it suitable for this purpose would be in the region of £12 "or possibly more." Even in those days £12 was not a lot of money – for instance, the cost of having a new bathing-box erected was something like £23 – so the work would not have been very extensive.

Even so, the council was divided on the issue - some members were reluctant to proceed with the work while others felt "they must provide proper bathing facilities." One councillor protested that they had already done so, pointing out that there was mixed bathing at the South Pier. However, one of his colleagues maintained that ladies who bathed at Murtagh's Mouth would not care about mixed bathing – in fact, some of them had objected.

To which the chairman responded: "Yes, we must have a separate place for them. We would destroy the interests of the town if we did not provide suitable bathing places for both sexes." At the end of the debate the clerk was asked to obtain tenders to have the work carried out.

A few years earlier, a sort of comic opera scenario developed at Murtagh's Mouth and again much of it was played

THE HIGH DIVE AT BLUE POOL, PORTRUSH

out at a meeting of the Urban Council in August, 1901. The council was considering a joint letter from two of their bathing-place attendants, James McAllister and Patrick McMichael complaining that although they had rented the South Pier and the Blue Pool bathing-places for the season, John Hopkins had, contrary to agreement, been allowed to open an opposition bathing place at the Salmon Rock, and on one day last week 18 ladies had bathed there.

The Council and Lord Antrim, who owned much of Portrush had been in dispute concerning bathing at the Salmon Rock (close to Murtagh's Mouth) and consequently the council had been forced to carry out improvements at the Blue Pool and provide additional bathing boxes. One councillor complained that Lord Antrim was "not acting nicely" in allowing the Salmon Rock to be again used by the ladies by a separate and distinct party.

Others questioned whether or not Lord Antrim knew anything about it, one of the councillors explaining that Hopkins anchored his boat in the bay and the ladies entered the water from it, not from the Salmon Rock.

The chairman's response to this was: "The Earl of Antrim stopped us, and he ought to stop him." Another comment was that "it only shows the long-headedness of Hopkins, in how he can out-manoeuvre Lord Antrim." Just how long this little boat bathing episode continued off the Salmon Rock is not clear but the decision the council came to after some further debate was that they had no power to interfere in the matter.

The attendants, who had to tender for the right to control the various bathing-places, were qualified instructors and lifeguards and on occasions they were called upon to exercise their lifesaving skills in real life rescues.

Mixed Bathing in the Harbour, Portrush

mysterious enchantment of the skerries

"...the firemen brought two bicycles
over to the islands and races were
staged on the grassy slopes."

T he idea of a picnic on the Skerry Islands would not be an appealing
proposition to many people today but believe it or not, 100 years ago
it was a different story. Each summer, for hundreds of holidaymakers,
these rugged and jagged looking islands, particularly the larger ones,
provided the ideal setting for a picnic and local boatmen were kept busy
rowing parties across the short stretch of water from the small Portandoo
harbour at Lansdowne.

An old record states that the Skerries "form the goal of a favourite jaunt by
picnickers, who go out to them in motor boats and rowing boats daily in
their hundreds." It also notes that the largest of the group of islands is
covered with soil that has been so honeycombed by rabbits that the grass
is springy underfoot." The back of the islands is a line of higher cliffs so that
the surface of the land facing south slopes gently to the sea forming a
sheltered suntrap.

The Skerries – at one time in the dim and distant past that was the name
by which Portrush was known – are as much a part of the rugged beauty
and charm of this part of the coastline as any of the more famous
landmarks. There are seventeen tiny islands or islets in the group, ranging
from a cluster known as the Otter Isles to the larger Winkle Island, Castle
Island and Island Barton. They are all uninhabited of course but from time

immemorial they have been a sanctuary for birds. Barnacle geese flourish there and Eider duck and Herring gull breed in safety.

"Anyone who is interested in bird life will find the Skerries a fascinating spot, for here seabirds of all kinds build their nests and are so numerous that one has to walk carefully in parts to avoid treading on the eggs or the young," was the advice given by one intrepid explorer early in the last century. Another little piece of ornithological history relating to the Skerries is worth recalling; these islands were, it is believed, the last nesting place in Western Europe of the Great Auk, now extinct. The reason for this is thought to have something to do with the bird's ungainly build; they found the rocky contours comparatively easy to land on.

The mysterious enchantment of the Skerries has long been an attraction for tourists, for most of whom a sea trip to the islands is a pleasant experience whether a landing is possible or not. Angling parties were sometimes landed for a day's fishing in the clear blue waters.

Down through the centuries the Skerry Roads have been known to mariners as a safe anchorage for ships and many a gale-lashed vessel owes its survival to the shelter of the islands.

Towards the end of the nineteenth century there was a good deal of support for a proposal to build a mammoth 'harbour of refuge' from the Skerries to the mainland, making it a port of call for the big ocean-going liners. One old record states: "Ophidian ambition contemplated the eclipse of the Port of Londonderry by joining up the Skerries to make a vast harbour, capturing all that port's trade and transforming Portrush into a metropolis overnight." But the project, estimated to cost £1 million, came to nothing.

Looking at the Skerries it is easy to conjure up tales of pirates, hidden treasure and ancient windjammers. Tradition has it that a once notorious pirate called Black Tavish is buried in an unmarked grave on the Skerries. Invaders from the Western Isles undoubtedly made frequent raids on the Ulster coast and this particular area bore the brunt of many of these forays because of its many natural landing places.

Black Tavish, it is said, was one of the most audacious of these raiders. It is believed that from the Skerries, which he made his base of operations, he and his pirates conducted a campaign of terror all along the coastline.

Today the calm of the islands is disturbed only by the endless growling of the sea, the plaintiff sounds of the wheeling gulls and the sibilant whisper of the wind in a hundred jagged clefts and crevices.

So it is even more incredible to think that on one occasion the local fire brigade were called to the islands, not to deal with any emergency but to enjoy themselves at their annual sports day! Precisely when this happened is a little obscure but it did happen. As part of the programme, sailing races were held to and from the Skerries and according to one old account the programme included an imposing line-up of events.

Apparently the firemen brought two bicycles over to the islands and races were staged over the grassy slopes – on which of the islands the historic bicycle race was staged is not mentioned. For sure it would have been a rough ride: "Unfortunately," this old account states, "the surface of the Skerries is rough owing to potatoes having once been planted there and in powering over these ridges, one competitor fell through the frame of the bicycle, putting an untimely end to the contest." Interestingly, it also mentions that swimming and diving in the Skerries pool were included as part of the sports day programme. And Joseph Sandford was named as the winner of the high jump.

For a good few years into the twentieth century, the challenge of swimming from the mainland to the Skerries was frequently attempted by both male and female swimmers with varying degrees of success. In the summer of 1912 one of these challenges was billed as a race and the contestants were named as Professor Barr from Glasgow, an expert swimmer, and a local man, Chris Varley. The race was from the Skerries to the Blue Pool.

However, it did not take place because Professor Barr did not turn up on the appointed day, much to the disappointment of a huge crowd of spectators who had gathered at the Blue Pool and other vantage points to witness the contest. In the circumstances, Varley, a well-known bandsman and who was also a wrestler, decided to go it alone. He proceeded to the Skerries in a boat with James Martin, the genial attendant at the Blue Pool. Another boat also accompanied him.

A reporter who witnessed the attempt wrote: "On this occasion Varley found his swim from the Skerries to the Blue Pool much harder than his attempt last year, owing to the fact that he now aimed at swimming in a straight line, and the currents, which were very strong, were almost too much for him. But he stuck pluckily to his task, and reached the Blue Pool, amid hearty plaudits, one hour and eleven minutes after the start."

Earlier that summer a Scottish visitor, a Miss Livingstone, swam from the Skerries to the mainland, a distance of about two miles and she completed the feat in spite of choppy seas. Her time of just over an hour, however, was much slower than the record for the swim which had been set some three years earlier by two lady swimmers, Miss Lizzie Lyons, Portrush and

Miss Eileen Campbell, Dungiven. Miss Lyons completed the distance in just 42 minutes and Miss Campbell in 52 minutes.

A brave attempt to swim to the Skerries and back was made in August, 1913 by J.A. Greenfield, a young Glasgow visitor who was both deaf and dumb. The first leg of the swim was completed successfully but unfortunately on the way back he was overcome by a bout of sea sickness and had to give up the attempt. "He is an intrepid swimmer," it was noted, "and it is a pity that the termination of his holidays prevented him from making a second attempt, otherwise he might have been successful and so have established a record for future swimmers to eclipse."

Just a couple of weeks later that marathon swim was achieved by a lady from Belfast, a Miss Cody, who was on holiday in Portrush. She swam to the Skerries and back in a time of just under two hours, a remarkably fine performance. She must have been an exceptionally strong swimmer because, in the words of a spectator, when she left the water "she seemed as if she could have repeated the performance."

The Skerry Roads... a safe anchorage for
ships down through the years

on the
old
windjammers

*"...the anchor plunged back into the sea
with one of the sailors clinging to it."*

A century ago there were still a few old time sailing ships, or windjammers as they were sometimes known, to be seen tied up at Portrush harbour and stately looking vessels they were, always attracting a good deal of interest from holidaymakers.

Few, if any, would have been aware of the remarkable story of a young Portrush lad and his thrilling adventures on one of these old vessels. What's more, he was just 12 years old when he went to sea, joining the crew on one of the old high-masted sailing ships. Later, as an old man, he recalled his adventures in a Press interview and because of the town's long seafaring history, it's worth recounting here.

In those days a sailor's life before the mast could be harsh and dangerous at times, particularly on transatlantic crossings. Although some would have carried a few passengers, mostly they were cargo vessels following well established trading routes.

In the middle of the nineteenth century Portrush was a small but nevertheless important port of call for the old windjammers – sometimes up to a dozen of these vessels could be seen anchored in the bay and frequently a few would be tied up in the harbour.

A vivid insight into that fascinating era is given in that interview with the old sailor in which he was referred to simply as 'the old bo'sun' as he looked back on his career at sea, spanned 30 years, as an able seaman. So we do not know who he was but I hope that somewhere in the archives of the town's seafaring history his name and his memory have been recorded for posterity.

He was 78 years old when he gave the interview and in it he recalled how, as an apprentice, he had joined the crew of the 'Emily Walters' on a voyage from Portrush to Newfoundland with a cargo of coal. He could still remember his first day at sea, not too surprising, perhaps, because it turned out to be quite an eventful day, to put it mildly.

This is how the story unfolds: "One day out from Portrush, the anchor was being heaved aboard. A seaman went down the side with a tackle which he fastened to the anchor. The line was not long enough; a second man climbed down the rope with another tackle to hook to the first. The two lines took the strain and the crew got ready to haul in. But the mate 'surged,' or slackened, the rope for a fraction of a second and the anchor plunged back into the sea with one of the sailors clinging to it. At this point the Captain of the ship took a hand. He seized a coil of rope and threw it to the man who, because of the heavy sea boots he was wearing, was having difficulty keeping afloat. Unfortunately, the heavy rope stuck the man on the head, stunning him and although a second rope was thrown, the struggling sailor, still dazed, was not able to grasp hold of it.

What happened next was surely a most cruel twist of fate. This is how it was recorded in the interview: "His sea boots were full of air and they rose to the surface, forcing the man's head under water. Before the eyes of the crew, while the ship raced on, their shipmate disappeared, but his boots stuck up like periscopes for a moment and then slowly followed him to his watery grave. It would be over two months before his wife learned that she had been widowed"

.

It must have been a harrowing sight for the crew to witness and particularly for the young apprentice. No doubt it was something he thought about often on that voyage to Newfoundland which would take just over a month. The experience did not turn him against the sea, however, because he would spend the next 30 years sailing the oceans of the world in those tall-masted ships, eventually becoming a bo'sun. 'Learning the ropes' was something which had to be tackled, quite literally, on board those full-rigged sailing ships, often carrying over 30 sails, so the ropes needed to attach them to the rigging would often be tangled and hard to identify.

As another old newspaper report pointed out: "Yet a sailor on a windjammer knew how to make or mend any of the sails and could go straight to any rope, even in the dark of night. The bo'sun went aloft every day and inspected every foot of the rigging to see that all was trim and true; anything that was not was immediately repaired. At the head of each mast were the sky-sails, and below them the royals, the top-gallants, the top-sails and the fore-sails in succession."

In those days, seamen who joined their ships at Portrush were financially better off – they were paid higher wages than on a ship sailing out of Belfast. As a general rule they could expect to earn ten shillings a month more on a Portrush ship. An able seaman was usually paid two pounds and ten shillings a month, or two pounds a month if it was for a long voyage to the United States or South America.

It was hard-earned money, especially when a storm blew up and it was a case of all hands on deck, which would be often swamped by huge waves. The old bo'sun from Portrush recalled one such occasion when, because of rough seas, the Captain decided to 'run before the gale.' He remembered it like this: "As we raced towards the southern Irish coast we found ourselves in company with an Italian ship, also running before the wind.

"On New Year's night we made the port of Waterford, but the Italian vessel carried on towards Fleetwood. She never reached it. On New Year's morning she ran aground on the Hook of Waterford and was lost with all hands."

Such was the hard life and times of a sailor in the days of the old sailing ships and it's fascinating to think that not only the old bosun but also many other Portrush men would have sailed on them to the far corners of the world, sometimes being away from home and family for months at a time.

Old sailing ships in the harbour

- MAURICE SPALECE -

Lifeboat Launched in a sea of Flowers!

"...she was pitched high on the towering crest of a wave, in a moment to be buried in the succeeding trough."

In the old days, during the busy summer months, Portrush lifeboat was itself something of a tourist attraction and this was very important from a fund-raising point of view.

The launch of the lifeboat was a big draw for thousands of visitors over the summer season and apart from the funds which it generated, it also provided good practice for the life-boatmen.

One of the most exciting of these old time launches took place in August, 1901, when a north-westerly gale was blowing. This launch was not just for the benefit of tourists but was the quarterly practice for the lifeboat crew and it took place "in weather well calculated to try the seaworthy qualities of the stoutest boat as well as the nerves of the most experienced boatmen."

A heavy sea was running before the gale when the lifeboat was launched from the slip under the command of Commander Holmes, R.N., the divisional inspector, with the following crew: Thomas Patton (coxswain), James Davis (second coxswain), Archibald McFarlane, James Martin, jun., Charles McAllister, jun., John Hopkins, jun., Robert Elkin, William McShannock, Charles McCulloch, James Martin, sen., W.J. Bacon, Dr. Porter and Jas. Woodside.

"Large crowds of interested spectators watched the practice of the boat in the bay," it was reported, "holding their breath as she was pitched high on the towering crest of a wave, in a moment to be buried in the succeeding trough."

The practice session lasted for an hour, so there would have been many gasps of breath from those watching from the shore before the lifeboat was beached on the East Strand, "the run before the wind constituting the most absorbing spectacle of the day."

In those days the lifeboat was housed in a building at Lansdowne and it was launched down a steep incline into the open sea, a spectacle both exciting and dramatic to witness, even on a calm day, so there was always a large crowd of spectators.

In the summer of 1913, to mark "Lifeboat Day", the lifeboat was duly launched but on this occasion the fund-raising efforts were slightly different – it was very much a case of "saying it with flowers." A flower-selling campaign had been organised to coincide with the event and the flower-sellers were a persuasive band of local and visiting ladies.

A substantial sum was raised in support of the worthy cause. It was reported: "Judging by the number of little blue cornflower buttonholes – it, by the way, is the one adopted by the Institution as its permanent flower – which one encountered almost everywhere, thousands must have been sold." The buttonholes cost two-pence and those who yielded to the "entreaties of the engaging young ladies" had the additional satisfaction of knowing that they were helping a good cause.

The launch did not take place until the afternoon when "a crowd of remarkable dimensions" gathered in the vicinity of the Lifeboat Station. It must indeed have been a spectacle because at that time the lifeboat was the "Hopwood," the last "pulling and sailing" lifeboat to be stationed at Portrush. It remained in service until 1924 when it was replaced with the first motorised lifeboat.

The Coxswain of the Hopwood on that launch was Jack Stewart and he and his crew had everything in spick and span order. This is a description of the launching: "The lifeboat glided down the well greased ways and into the water as graceful as a swan, to the accompaniment of a salvo of cheering from those on shore. The crew rowed to the Skerries and back to the station, where the boat was safely housed."

Sometimes, if the sea was rough, it would not be possible to bring the boat back to the station and in those circumstances it would usually be brought into the harbour. From there it was beached and, with the assistance of volunteers, would be hauled along the streets down to the Lansdowne station. Sometimes it would be loaded onto the back of a lorry and driven to the station. During its time at Portrush, the Hopwood and the gallant crews who manned her, were responsible for saving 23 lives.

For some reason or other, it was always ladies who took up the collection on launch days so, just for the record, some of their names are being recorded here. These were the ladies who displayed so much flower power on that special occasion in the summer of 1913: Mrs John Claudius Beresford, Miss Beresford, Miss Bullock, Miss Beckett, Miss Gladys Boyd, Miss Carlyle, Miss C. Campbell, Miss M. Campbell, Miss H. Crawford, Miss Eagleson, Miss Hunt, Miss Lavell, Miss Motherwell, Miss C. Motherwell, Miss McCullagh, Miss O'Neill, Miss Reid, Miss Roe, Miss Scott and Miss Walker. They were assisted by Masters Billy Richardson and R. McMorris.

Rescue by Breeches Buoy

A year earlier, at another launching ceremony, this time under the command of Coxswain Thomas Patton, it was reported that the boat, manned by a stalwart crew, glided gracefully down the well greased ways and took the water amid a round of applause from the hundreds of onlookers. The report continued: "After making a short cruise round the Skerries, the Hopwood proceeded towards the bay at Portstewart and returned to Portrush harbour, being subsequently conveyed to the lifeboat station."

Unusually, during the preparations for that particular launch, one of the local pierrot troupes had given "an enjoyable performance in aid of the noble institution" and a collection taken up which realised the sum of £9-2s-1d., a princely sum, no doubt, in those days.

An interesting historical note about the Hopwood lifeboat: it was built by the Thames Iron Works Company and arrived in Portrush in August, 1902 to replace the old lifeboat, the "Robert and Agnes Blair." It was of the Liverpool type, 35 feet long, 10 feet wide and rowing 12 oars double banked. She had two sliding, or drop, keels to increase her seaworthiness while in deep water without diminishing the effectiveness of the flat bottom and light draught which was necessary when in shallow water.

The cost of the new boat and equipment had been met by a legacy bequeathed to the Institution by Samuel Weymouth Hopwood, of Queen Anne's Mansions, London for the building and equipping of a lifeboat which would bear his name.

At that time some 36 lifeboats were stationed at various locations around the coast of Ireland and needless to say they were kept busy particularly during the winter months. In 1901 the cost of maintaining the Irish lifeboat stations amounted to £6,600.

In August, 1912, another little bit of lifesaving history was made in Portrush when it was announced that a company of local men had formed themselves into a volunteer party to operate rocket lifesaving apparatus supplied by the Board of Trade and which had been recently located at the Dock Head entrance of Ramore Hill. Here a station had been erected for the storage of the apparatus.

The old Lifeboat Station.

The rocket device solved the problem of how to get a heavy rope onto a stranded vessel in order to rescue the crew. It worked on the principle that a rocket fired from the shore with a thin line attached could then be used to haul a much heavier rope onto the stricken vessel. Once it was  made fast, a pulley and what was known as a bosun's chair, could be attached and used to winch the crew back to land. Later it became known as the Breeches Buoy, a life-ring or harness that was more secure.

By all accounts, the Portrush volunteers acquitted themselves well on their first training session on Ramore Hill, inspectors from the Board of Trade and Coastguard officers expressing themselves as highly satisfied with their performance. The volunteers were under the direction of Chief Officer Waite of the local Coastguard Station and afterwards he paid this tribute: "With a first-class lifeboat and a brave and trustworthy crew, and a plucky and competent company of men ready to work the rocket apparatus, we feel confident that the Portrush men will render a good account of themselves whenever their services may be required."

A few months earlier, the tragic fate of the Titanic touched the hearts of everyone who heard the sad news, but particularly women because of the heroic behaviour of the crew of the great ship in ensuring that women and children were given preference when the lifeboats were launched.

In Portrush, a successful appeal was organised by women in support of a fund which had been set up by the Daily Mail on behalf of the survivors. It was led by Miss Hamilton, then chairman of the local Urban Council. She had issued an appeal to the women of the town "on behalf of the bereaved families of the heroic men who calmly met their death in order that the women and children on board the ill-fated liner might be saved."

A news item on the outcome of the appeal stated: "From Saturday to Wednesday a collecting box was placed outside the White House in which the sum of £11.10s. was collected and forwarded to the Daily Mail's Women's Fund."

In sending the subscription, Miss Hamilton, whose family owned the White House, wrote: "The women of Portrush would like to join with their sisters in England in paying tribute to the memory of those brave men on board the Titanic who stood aside and willingly accepted death that the women and children might live, who gave their lives for others, the rich for the poor and the strong for the weak, and in so doing proved themselves true sons of God and men worthy of a niche in the nation's most sacred memories. No woman can read the account of the awful tragedy and the brave self-sacrifice with untouched heart. We send you a small sum to be added to the fund which is being got up for the benefit of the homes now fatherless, in memory of the men who gave up their lives."

It was a touching tribute and one which gives yet another insight into the great sea tragedy which is still talked about today.

Loss of the Titanic - a Portrush appeal.

mina's historic "dip" in the harbour

"…she was by then one of the fastest lady swimmers in the world."

The story of a young lady from Australia who "took a dip" in the harbour at Portrush in the summer of 1912 shortly after she had made history by winning a silver medal for swimming at the Olympic Games in Stockholm that year, has never been told – until now.

It is only now that the story has come to light and it came about quite by chance as I was delving into some dusty old records as part of the research for this book. So I suppose you could describe it as a little historical "scoop," to use an old journalistic cliché. It's a discovery, I must admit, that has given me immense pleasure and satisfaction.

I wanted to write a little piece about diving and swimming in Portrush in the early part of the last century. At that time, and indeed for many years afterwards, organised displays at the harbour and the Blue Pool, were hugely popular events in the holiday entertainment programme.

I did not really expect, however, to come across such a little gem, even though the dip which 21-year-old Mina Wylie took in the harbour that summer day all those years ago, was simply for her own enjoyment and was not part of any organised display. As it turned out, she gave a stunning solo performance and the strange thing is that although there were plenty of people about, no one who witnessed her amazing prowess in the water seems to have had any idea who she was.

Even the attendant at the harbour bathing place, James McAlister, who would have seen many fine divers and swimmers in his time, did not realise that this young lady was a superstar in the world of competitive swimming.

This is the full text of the news item which recorded her presence in Portrush: "Among the visitors during the week was a Miss Wylie from Australia who surprised those who were fortunate enough to see her take a dip in the harbour on Tuesday. Miss Wylie showed herself an expert in the water in all styles of swimming and diving which were marvellous. The popular attendant, Jamie, says her power and grace in the water was simply astonishing and her speed in swimming better than anything he had ever seen."

That was not surprising because Mina Wylie was by then officially one of the two fastest women swimmers in the world, second only to fellow Australian and good friend, Fanny Durack, who had won a Gold medal at the Stockholm Olympics, beating Mina by the narrowest of margins.

The reason for her visit to Northern Ireland is easily explained as it turns out. She was accompanied by her father, Henry, who was also with her in Stockholm. He was born in Belfast and had gone to Australia as a young man. So they had come to look up some relatives – in her personal diary Mina noted that they had also visited Bangor, where she also had a swim, and Portrush. She wrote that while in Portrush she "had a swim" followed by dinner (perhaps in the Northern Counties Hotel?). The following day she and her father went to the Giant's Causeway, making the journey by the electric tram, and before leaving Portrush they also took a trip in a jaunting-car.

Perhaps it was not too surprising that no one recognised this world champion swimmer because as a report in the Belfast Evening Telegraph noted, their visit was "more or less of a private character." However, the Telegraph report did not mention anything about her Portrush visit.

Mina's diary records her Portrush visit.

News from the Stockholm Olympics had been reported in the local newspapers but there were no photographs and the coverage was mostly listing results in the various sporting events. So although Mina Wylie, by becoming the first Australian woman to win a silver medal in Olympic swimming, had carved for herself a unique place in sporting history, she remained, outside her own country, comparatively unknown.

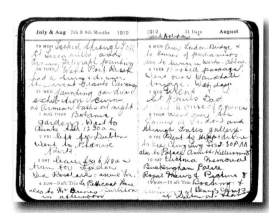

Her journey to fame is certainly a fascinating one and because of her previously unknown link with Portrush, it is worth recalling here. Even as a five-year-old she was a gifted swimmer and so much at home in the water that she could swim with her hands and feet tied. Along with her father and brothers she took part in exhibitions of "trick and fancy swimming" at Sydney harbour carnivals.

Henry Wylie was a well-known figure in Sydney and his prowess as a swimmer was formidable. He achieved fame as an under-water swimmer, winning the Australian Championship by swimming under-water over a distance of 92 yards in 1896. That form of competition did not last long and it was banned by the medical profession.

As a teenager, Mina and her great rival, Fanny Durack, dominated swimming in Australia for several years leading up to the Stockholm Olympics in 1912 and there was growing public demand that they should be allowed to compete. As a result of this, the New South Wales Ladies Amateur Swimming Association changed the rule which forbade their members to appear in competitions when men were present. And so they became the first Australian women to compete in swimming events at the Olympics.

Mina also competed in the New South Wales and Australian championships from 1906 to 1934, winning no fewer than 115 titles, including every Australian and New South Wales championship in freestyle, backstroke and breaststroke. She was inducted into the International Swimming Hall of Fame in 1975.

One cannot help thinking that had the news got out that an Olympic swimming champion, an attractive young lady, was in Portrush and would be taking a dip in the harbour, thousands of spectators would have turned up and, in the words of Jamie, the harbour bathing-place attendant, would have witnessed a truly astonishing display of swimming and diving. And it wouldn't have cost them a penny!

Mina Wylie, who not only won a medal but also made history at the Olympics in Stockholm in 1912, had a long and no doubt interesting life, living to the ripe old age of 93. She died in July, 1984.

By a strange coincidence, she was not the only Olympic swimmer to be seen in action at Portrush harbour that summer. Towards the end of August a gentleman named Hadden Tilsley, from Leicestershire, who had represented England in the 1908 Olympics, was in Portrush. He held various championship titles from the English Midland counties and reached the pinnacle of his career when he was selected for the Olympics. The short news report of his visit simply added that "he is at present spending his holidays in Portrush."

splashing out
at the white rocks

*"They dried themselves afterwards by
sprinting naked along the strand."*

Just over l00 years ago, the game of caman (a cross between hockey and hurling) was played in Portrush and according to one old record there was a tradition that a match was played between two local teams on Christmas Day. There was another tradition, it seems, that after the match the players scrambled onto the beach for a quick dip in the cold Atlantic – but it was a dip with a difference.

The contestants would strip "to the altogether", as one old-time correspondent put it, and race into the waves to finish off their endeavours on the sporting field. Writing in 1914, this is how he recalled the event:

"Could you imagine a game of caman on the Portrush golf links today? Yet it is not so very many years since the present course, in the vicinity of the White Rocks, was the scene of an annual encounter on Christmas Day.

"A gentleman who took part in these exhilarating and often sanguinary competitions stated that after the match was over the contestants used to strip to the altogether in the snow-covered sand hills and plunge into the icy water for a swim.

"They dried themselves afterwards by sprinting naked along the strand. It was very healthy and invigorating and all the rest of it, no doubt, but for our own part we would prefer our bath-room every time. What do you think?"

I wonder what people did think of such capers in those fairly prim and proper days? And what about the spectators, if there were any? Perhaps they were banned from the post-match celebrations. It's the first time I've heard of this old tradition and I would be inclined to treat it with a little bit of scepticism in the absence of more corroborating information. At any rate, it's an amusing tale and one which adds to the aura and romance of the seaside in the olden days.

And speaking of seaside romance, the writer of a humorous piece entitled "Holiday Vagaries" waxed eloquently on the subject. He wrote: "If a man – almost any unattached male will do – wishes to feel the joys of being sought after and an object of general female attention, let him hasten away to the seaside. What gay and girlish groups will be formed about him! How they will laugh at his jokes and listen with awe to his opinions! With what warmth they will admire his atrocious ties and homicidal socks – the colours are so striking and becoming, you know. They may even sit still while he sings…"

When it came to the crunch, however, it seems that the girls were well able to handle the boys, as this further extract explains: "We have walked with them, and read poetry to them, and eaten ice-cream with them, and discussed with them whether marriage was possible where true love was not. We have even proposed to – but we must not carry these confidences too far. Suffice it to state that even those who accepted us let us see clearly that they regarded the eternal affection we swore to one another as being subject to recall with due notice. Sometimes they didn't even bother to give us the notice!"

In another report on the same subject, a slightly different "take" on the whole question of seaside romances was outlined: "Summer seems to describe anything which is delightful and fleeting, from friends to flirtations. Some of the many gallant speeches now being taken out and aired for the season may mean a more serious ending than a summer philandering but most of them are as quickly forgotten as the June roses.

"Once in a while the summer flirtation becomes a lasting attachment, to be followed by a wedding in the spring. There is a story to the effect that at a certain summer resort where, among the guests, there were seven girls and seven young men, there were to be found forty-nine engaged couples. This may be mathematics, but it looks like the compound fractions of Cupid's school."

"Singing amorous madrigals by moonlight" is another romantic line taken from a periodical of the time, in an article on the same subject, although just how widely practised this was in Portrush, if at all, is a matter of conjecture but the writer paints a nice picture and puts it in context like this: "…the general plans, the vague and glowing dreams – ah! the pictures of oneself poised like a god in the path of the breakers while the peaches on the beaches gaze longingly upon one, or again singing amorous madrigals by moonlight – these visions are well worth the disillusion that follows."

The White Rocks was a favourite location for picnics in the early part of the last century and according to one old tradition, they were on a grand scale. And there was probably more than a hint of romance in the air as well because some were organised, in turn, by the young ladies and the young men of the town.

This is one reference I came across: "…the young ladies of the town invited the young men to a picnic at the White Rocks in return for one given by the latter a few weeks previously. The main body of the pleasure-seekers left the promenade about 2 p.m., not in the least disheartened by the threatening rain clouds. Soon the rendezvous was reached and the male helpers quickly had a fire lighted and the boiler ready."

There were about eighty people in the party "young men and maidens, hungry and gay." It was hard work for the ladies who were in charge but there was plenty of food and it went down well; the picnic baskets were "a good deal lighter" when everyone had been fed.

Then followed a programme of fun and games with "various members of the party rendering a selection of humorous songs" and afterwards everyone was said to have had "a high old time on the sands." This is how it was described: "There were races for men and races for women, prizes at once useful and ornamental being given through the generosity of a few of the sterner sex. Then there was dancing to the music of a mouth-organ, the sweet strains of which brought the rabbits of the neighbouring warren in amazement to the mouths of their burrows." After the dancing, more beach games were enjoyed and then, about eight o'clock in the evening "all sat down again in a grassy dell to a second helping of milk and cakes with fruit."

A hearty vote of thanks was proposed to the ladies for the splendid outing and it all finished up with the singing of "Auld Lang Syne," the party arriving back in town about an hour later.

The success of the picnic was due in no small measure to "the liberality of the ladies," so much so that a second picnic was organised a week later in order to dispose of the surplus cakes and fruit. Plans were already being made by the young men for a return picnic at the end of the summer; they would not be behind, it was stated, in the matter of entertaining.

Doubtless those old picnics led to a few romantic liaisons. It would be interesting to know just how long that old tradition lasted.

transport of delight

-MAURICE McALEESE-

*"With so many trips it was inevitable,
perhaps, that things didn't always run smoothly."*

For many people, one of the great pleasures of a visit to Portrush in the early years of the last century was to experience a trip on the old tram which plied between the town and the Giant's Causeway. By then it had been running for about a quarter of a century, going from strength to strength and adding considerably to the charms and delights of Portrush as a holiday destination.

Most visitors to Portrush did not leave without making the tram journey to the Causeway at least once. The track skirted some spectacular coastal scenery en route, notably the White Rocks and Dunluce Castle, and depending on the weather one could opt for either an open-air carriage or an enclosed one.

Some of the tram drivers were well versed in local history and passengers might be given little snapshots from the past, particularly if the tram stopped at Dunluce, which it frequently did, to allow passengers a more prolonged view of the old castle. Markets and fairs were formerly held at Dunluce and right up to the end of the eighteenth century they continued to be held in November each year. They were then held at Bushmills because they had become "a depot for rioting, gambling, drinking and sundry other vices."

The magnetic pull of the old Causeway tram is strikingly illustrated in one small statistic dating back to a July day in 1913 when no fewer than 3,200 passengers passed over the line, creating a record for the tramway. Now that's impressive!

That summer it was reported that traffic on the electric tramway had been exceptionally good. "All the available cars," it was announced, " have been steadily on the move, conveying crowds of holidaymakers to and from the Giant's Causeway."

And many compliments were paid to Mr. W.A. Traill, C.E. and the manager, Mr. Daniel Fall, who were "assiduous in looking after the comfort and safety of the passengers".

The line was so busy that in the course of one week the tramcars had been carrying about 2,500 passengers each day. With so many trips, it was inevitable, perhaps, that things didn't always run smoothly on the narrow tramway lines. This was not necessarily seen as a drawback but was described in a newspaper article as adding to the excitement of the journey. This is how it was put:

"Conductors at this season of the year have many exciting experiences owing to negligence of persons passing over the tramway line. On Wednesday last a man belonging to Coleraine, who was in charge of a horse and van, had a narrow escape when emerging from the laneway leading from Dunluce Castle. The bell was sounded but the horse was just about to be driven over the line in front of the tram when Mr. Samuel Campbell, who was in charge, instantly applied the brakes and stopped the car, thereby averting a serious collision."

Also reported that summer was an incident in which a small pony and trap collided with the tram opposite the railway station. Again it was a case of a narrow escape because the pony was only slightly injured in its forelegs while the occupants of the trap were unhurt.

On yet another occasion, the tram was involved in an incident described as "alarming" and this time it happened in the centre of the town at the junction of Causeway Street and Main Street. Again, the incident made the local newspapers: "A Ford four-seater motor-car belonging to and driven by Mr. James McCurdy, cycle manufacturer, Portstewart, collided with the crowded 3.15 pm tram from Portrush station.

An old Tramway ticket

"Streams of people were then passing along Main Street, and the tram was rounding the corner very slowly. Mr. McCurdy, who had two ladies and a gentleman passenger in his car, was returning from the Causeway. On reaching the corner he observed the tram and the crowd, and in endeavouring to get clear of both, the car struck the tram, which the conductor promptly brought to a standstill.

"The occupants of the motor luckily escaped injury. When the car was extricated it was found that the radiator and the glass screen were smashed, and a lamp, mudguard and footboard slightly damaged. The tram proceeded to Bushmills and the Causeway and the motor-car was pushed along to a motor garage."

An accident which could have had very serious consequences involved one of the drivers, Mr. Samuel Campbell. He was at the controls on his way to the Causeway when shortly after passing Dunluce the brake slipped and, swinging round, struck him sharply on the forearm. The brake was like a large handlebar beside the controls. Mr. Campbell, although suffering great pain, remained at the controls. One account of the incident states: "... he would not give in and actually brought the tram to the Causeway and back to Bushmills before he could be persuaded by his comrades to leave what he considered his post of duty." Later he was examined by a doctor and it was found that his arm was badly broken below the elbow.

Those were all minor incidents compared to the tragedy which occurred in the summer of 1903 involving the deaths of two children. This extract from the company's annual meeting describes what happened: "Two children lay down on the bank of the line at a curve where they could easily have been seen if standing, and fell asleep, and waking up suddenly after the engine had passed them were killed by the car following."

The Company was not held to blame for the accident at the coroner's inquest which followed. However, an action for damages was taken by the parents of the children and although having no legal responsibility, the Company, it was reported "thought it best to settle the case for £75..."

That was not the only litigation involving the company that year. They were met with a claim from a passenger who had been removed from a first-class covered carriage which he had occupied on a wet day on a return journey from the Causeway though having only a third class ticket. A report presented at the annual meeting continued: "One would have expected that the first duty of the Company was to give the first-class seats to those who held first-class tickets, even though the others should offer to pay the excess fare, but a judge and a Belfast jury held that the law is "first come, first served" and so the Company was mulcted in £25 damages and costs."

Almost four decades on from that record-breaking summer in Portrush, the old Causeway tram made its last sad journey – that was back in 1949. Many people felt that it should have been preserved on the grounds that it would have continued to be a major tourist attraction for the area. Having grown up in Portrush, I remember that little piece of history well and I later wrote about it. One of the pieces I wrote was a sort of obituary for the old tram but I like to think of it as my own personal tribute to the men and women who worked for the company and for the comfort and safety of the passengers. And as a tribute too, of course, to Mr. William Traill, the man who made the dream come true. It's in the next chapter.

tramway "secret" revealed

*"He allowed me to stand beside him as he drove
the tram on a special day-trip to the Causeway."*

Back in the summer of 1949 I was just old enough to appreciate that something momentous was about to happen in our small town. For weeks there had been talk that the old tramway, which was such a vital part of our community life, was to be scrapped and when it finally did happen, it cast an air of gloom and despondency over the whole town.

I could hardly believe that the quaint old tram would never run again, that a mode of transport which, for me at any rate, had a mystical, magical aura about it, would be no more. Even now, after the passing of so many years, I still think back nostalgically to those joyful days, especially if I'm caught in a traffic jam or waiting in a crowded airport lounge for a delayed flight.

When the last tram rumbled along the eight mile stretch of line from Portrush to the Causeway, which I was assured was the Eighth Wonder of the World, it was like saying goodbye to an old friend. That day sticks out in my memory: it seemed as if the whole town had turned out to witness the last sad journey. I stood and watched from the front porch of our house in Causeway Street and I don't mind admitting that there was a tear in my eye as the old tram, filled with passengers, trundled on its way to the scrapyard and oblivion.

Our house was close to the tramway lines and ever since I could remember, the rumble of heavy iron wheels on the track had been music to my ears.

It was a vibrant, living sound and I fancied the old tram was talking to me in a secret, rhythmic language that only I could understand.

One of the drivers was a gentleman called Mr. Scott, who happened to be a friend of my father's, and sometimes when the tram was passing our house, Mr. Scott would sound the big brass alarm bell, not because of any emergency, but by way of a salute. It was as if it was a signal for my father to check his watch, which he always did, to see if the tram was keeping to its schedule: more often than not it was dead on time.

It was because of this friendship with my father that on one occasion Mr. Scott, a portly gentleman with a large bushy moustache, who looked as if he had been tailor-made for the job, allowed me to stand beside him as he drove the tram on a special day-trip to the Causeway and although we passed some of the most spectacular scenery en route, I could not take my eyes off the bright, highly polished controls.

The array of shiny brass knobs and handles was truly impressive and I marvelled at the ease with which Mr. Scott, with his big, clumsy looking hands, manipulated them to keep the tram running at a smooth and steady pace. Occasionally he would glance down at me and smile approvingly at the enthralled expression on my face.

For safety reasons, the tram had to maintain a sedate speed while in the precincts of the town, making it easy for adventure-seeking youngsters like myself, oblivious to all danger, to steal a ride by jumping onto the footboard of the end carriage, particularly if there were not many passengers on board. However, the sharp-eyed conductor was always on the look-out for young "stowaways" and so I confined my errant ways to simply clinging onto a more concealed ledge at the back of the last carriage for a few fleeting, but wildly ecstatic moments, usually on my way to and from school.

Years later, when I became a journalist and started delving into aspects of local history, I discovered that the tramway had been built mainly due to the imagination and initiative of one man, William Acheson Traill, surely one of the unsung heroes in the annals of public transport.

He managed to surmount incredible hurdles of public protest and bureaucratic wrangling to pave the way for his dream feat of engineering, giving this tiny corner of Ireland a new and revolutionary form of transport.

Officially opened in 1883, it was the first hydro-electric railway in the world – the first to use electricity generated by water power.

On September 21, 1881 when the first sod was cut to mark the start of the historic project, the London correspondent of the Daily Express wrote: "It is greatly to the credit of all concerned that Ulster is taking the lead of England and Scotland in testing this new means of propulsion…Before long tourists may hope to be carried to the far-famed Causeway on the wings of electricity. It is confidently believed that the application of the dynamo-electricity power to railways cannot be long delayed."

I've since learned of a "secret" concerning the Causeway tram that was kept for 30 years. It had to do with a last minute hitch on the memorable day of the inaugural run - and how it almost didn't happen!

Only Mr Traill and his close associates knew about the drama that had unfolded that day and he did not reveal it until some three decades later while he was addressing a party of engineers on a visit to the Causeway. Members of the Junior Institution of Engineers "and their lady friends," were the first to hear the story which, until then, had remained untold.

This is taken from a news report of the engineers' visit that day in July, 1910: "In 1883 things were very different from what they are now. They had no proper insulated cables; in fact, they had no proper means of insulating anything, and what they adopted was a side conducting rail which they had to insulate as best they could. In the connecting rail there were a number of gaps leading into fields along the way, and these had to be connected with insulating cables underneath."

At the Tramway depot

The problem, it was explained, was that these first cables were constantly breaking down. There were sixty altogether so in order to make sure that all were working perfectly for the opening, they had to be checked and repairs, if needed, carried out as quickly as possible. Even so, it was a last minute rush, the last six faulty cables only being repaired on the day of the inaugural run.

That was not all. There had been a delay also in connecting with the water-power from the River Bush at Bushmills to generate the electricity needed to run the tram. So as a standby, engineers had been using a temporary steam engine to drive the electric generators at the Portrush end. By the opening day, however, the hydro-electric power station on the River Bush was completed and working satisfactorily.

There was still more drama to come. While the party of distinguished guests were inspecting the original plant at the Portrush depot before continuing their journey to the Causeway, Mr. Traill received a telegram from his assistant at the generating station to the effect that a breakdown in the insulation had occurred somewhere along the line.

"Imagine my feelings," he told the young engineers, "at the prospect of the electric car not being able to move. I said nothing but thought a great deal!"

Fortunately, the car did start and reached Bushmills without mishap and so was born a new form of motive power, bringing into being the first hydro-electric railway in the world. It was the first time the story of that shaky start had been told in public.

The return journey to Portrush still had to be undertaken and the fault on the line had still not been detected so while the distinguished party was being entertained to lunch, the company's head electrician was dispatched to find the fault, which he located half-way to Portrush. It meant that only up to that point could the power for the return journey be water generated. From there the switch was made to the steam power generating the electricity at Portrush. And so smooth was the transition that no one knew anything about it.

Mr. Traill could look back on the drama of that historic day with good humour. "What a fiasco it would have been," he speculated, "had they been unable to start the tram and just how near they were to it few ever knew. The incident has never been told in public up to this moment."

Incidentally, the opening ceremony on that historic day in 1883 was performed by the Lord Lieutenant of Ireland, Lord Spencer and he was the great grandfather of Princess Diana.

Today, hardly a trace remains of this great pioneering enterprise, surely worthy of a plaque or a memorial of some description, to mark the achievement of William Acheson Traill, a gifted engineer and a very remarkable man.

Suffragettes and the "battle" of ramore hill

I n the long hot summer of 1913, Portrush was a prime target for the Irish Women's Suffrage Society and the suffragettes, as they were known, were a high-profile presence on the streets, selling their newspaper "Votes for Women."

At one open-air meeting, the Society chairwoman, a Mrs Bennett, explained: "...although on holiday, a suffragette always takes her work with her and the presence of so many visitors in Portrush is too good an opportunity of making converts to be lost." The open-air meeting passed off peacefully but that wasn't always the case – the previous summer a huge rally at Ramore Hill resulted in a mini riot, caused by "a large number of men and boys on mischief bent." But the troublemakers did not have things all their own way - a news report of the incident was headlined "Suffragettes use their fists."

"...it was evident that a lively time was in store for the speakers."

For weeks prior to that rally, the suffragettes had been mingling with the visitors and distributing literature in support of the cause – the rally had also been advertised in prominent parts of the town, mainly through chalking the details on walls. This is an extract from a report of the rally: "Young fellows were there in large numbers, and from the very commencement of the proceedings it was evident that a lively time was in store for the speakers".

The "young fellows" had apparently worked out their strategy of disruption because "batches of them squatted here and there among the crowd and their behaviour at first was somewhat amusing. But the fun and frolic was carried too far, and a rather exciting and reprehensible state of affairs marked the termination of the meeting."

Speakers from Belfast and Dublin had to endure a lot of heckling. This is a description of one such incident: "While Miss Stacke was addressing the meeting, an elderly man nearby was keeping up an annoying disruption by shouting at the top of his voice. The lady in the chair was heard calling on him to 'shut up.' The individual appeared to be much excited, waving his hat and shouting to the crowd. One suffragette struck at him with a parasol, and two or three other women, amid roars of laughter from the onlookers, tackled him with their fists and forced him to beat a retreat to the outskirts of the assemblage."

Things were far from calming down and there continued to be persistent interruption "through the singing of parodies and the shouting of unsympathetic remarks." Rather more seriously, it was reported that sods and other missiles were being flung about indiscriminately "some of them falling upon the heads and shoulders of the ladies and gentlemen, especially those adjacent to the speakers."

In spite of all this, the women attempted to carry on with the meeting and the speaker at this stage, Mrs Baker from Belfast a fluent and convincing speaker, described in a nutshell their aims and objects, claiming that women were putting principle before party in this great progressive movement. They would no longer submit, she said, to be the 'doormats' for men. If women were good enough to be the mothers of the sons of the nation, surely they were good enough to exercise the franchise, she declared.

She had struggled to be heard over a constant babble kept up by a number of young men and the noise became so great that at this point the meeting was brought to a close.

It had been presided over by a lady from Dublin, Miss N. Stacke, possibly a sister of the earlier speaker, and she is said to have done so "with a gracefulness of manner that repelled anything in the nature of serious interruption…" Obviously that state of affairs did not prevail for too long but before mayhem broke out she paid tribute to the people and visitors of Portrush for the support they had received over the last six weeks which showed that in this part of the world "progress was their watchword."

Later, it was announced that a lady who was descried as "one of the greatest forces in the women's suffrage movement" would be coming to Portrush to address a meeting in the Town Hall. Miss Alice Abadam from London had given "yeoman service in building up the cause and bringing it to the forefront of practical politics." In a Press release she was given a big build-up: "She speaks with a conviction born of knowledge acquired in working amongst the most destitute of women workers, and by self-sacrifice and personal service amongst them she has gained an indisputable right to speak of their sufferings. The movement which culminated in the passage of the Criminal Law Amendment Bill owes its strength and impetus, if not its initiation, more to her than anyone else."

It was stressed that the Society under which the meeting would be held, was non-militant. Perhaps that assurance would have prevented scenes similar to the ones at Ramore Hill on a day which has gone down on record as a day the suffragettes had to resort to fisticuffs and the wielding of parasols in order to defend themselves from the ignorant onslaught of some mischievous and misguided individuals.

Visit of a famous battleship

"Many were the exclamations of wonder and admiration at the sights which met the gaze of visitors at every turn."

I n the early summers of the last century, the sight of warships at anchor off the Skerry Roads was not all that unusual and, naturally enough, they attracted a lot of interest among visitors and townspeople.

It was something which the local Council was always keen to arrange with the Admiralty because such visits were of no small benefit to the local economy and were a huge tourist attraction; as one commentator noted, they "brought joy, and a good deal of money, to many people in the town."

The summer of 1907 was no exception but it was particularly noteworthy because one of the warships making a courtesy visit to Portrush in July was the gigantic – and as it turned out, ill fated – Armoured Cruiser, H.M.S. "Drake." Some 10 years later, the visit would be recalled sadly and poignantly by many of the townspeople and visitors who were able not only to view the ship from the shore but were also able to board her and be taken on conducted tours by members of the crew.

A veritable flotilla of small boats – and one paddle steamer, the "Royal Norman" - set out from the harbour to be given a close-up view of the Drake and although in the earlier part of the day, it was a Sunday, there had been some rain and a thick haze, in the evening the sun came out. Thus, according to one Press report "the crowds who made this shortest of sea voyages did so under pleasant auspices."

Another reporter wrote: "Being one of those who had to wait until Sunday for a holiday, I ran the risk of offending my Sabbatarian friends, and journeyed by rail and sea to view the cruiser. It wasn't a work of necessity; but my conscience stretched in proportion to my admiration for the British Navy. That's the best excuse I can make and I know it's not up to much!" A little bit of wrestling with the Sunday observance code for that gentleman of the Press. Nevertheless, he travelled in some comfort on board the Royal Norman out to the Drake and he declared that it was "an excellent means of getting across." In his report, he also made this observation: "Every available boat in the place was engaged in carrying interested sightseers to and fro, and sometimes they were loaded to an extent which made me thankful I had chosen the steamer."

Fortunately, there was a very calm sea that day so there were no mishaps. For the local fishermen who deployed their boats, it was a welcome boost to their incomes and they operated continuous trips throughout the day, mostly from the small Portandoo harbour.

The guided tours of the battleship were impressive. The same reporter wrote: "Too much could not be said of the opportunities and facilities which were accorded visitors in going over the 'Drake,' this magnificent leviathan of the deep. Many were the exclamations of wonder and admiration at the sights which met the gaze of visitors at every turn."

A nice tribute was paid to the crew, who were described as "models of civility and courtesy" and very willing to answer the many questions they were asked although, apparently, some of the sailors had quite a struggle to keep a straight face at some of the queries put to them. It was all summed up neatly in this little bit of journalistic scepticism : "I question, however, if after an elaborate explanation of the action of the guns and the other great and mysterious machinery of the boat, many of the visitors were much wiser when they came away."

The visitors may have been perplexed by the technicalities relating to guns and machinery but neither could they get their heads round the accommodation logistics for a crew of 900 men. "How they all stow away their hammocks and pick them out again, for one thing, caused some wonderment..."

Be that as it may, they had been given a unique insight into what life was like on board a British man-of-war and no doubt it would have been a topic of conversation for a long time afterwards.

That would have been especially so when they heard the news that the armoured cruiser had been torpedoed by a German U-boat off the north-west tip of Rathlin Island on the morning of October 2, 1917. Nineteen members of the crew were killed. The crippled cruiser remained afloat after the attack and was subsequently escorted into Church Bay by HMS Martin and other auxiliary ships. A short time later she listed badly, capsized and sank in 18 metres of water.

It was a sad end to a proud ship which had been in service since 1902 and which, in the summer of 1907, had provided so much pleasure and excitement for thousands of people while she lay at anchor in the peaceful waters of the Skerry Roads.

prime minister's
surprise visit

"On landing the visitors immediately
requisitioned a couple of jaunting-cars…"

T he Prime Minister then slung his golf bag over his shoulder and walked down to the harbour, accompanied by the other members of the party…

The Prime Minister was Herbert Asquith, the date was June, 1910 and it was Portrush harbour he was walking down to. He had just enjoyed a round of golf on the Royal Portrush links and, amazingly, only a small number of people had been aware of his visit. It was a very low-key affair – there appears to have been a total absence of security of any kind - even the local constabulary were taken by surprise. The headline in the local weekly newspaper, the Constitution, captured this: The Prime Minister at Portrush – A Surprise Visit.

However, as inevitably happens on these occasions, it was not possible to throw a cloak of secrecy over everything because, as you can imagine, the means of transport chosen by the Prime Minister to get to Portrush was far from conventional.

He and his golfing companions, who included the First Lord of the Admiralty, arrived in some style aboard the Admiralty special service vessel, intriguingly named "Enchantress." This is what one reporter wrote: "The news of the visit travelled slowly, and the great majority of the residents did not become aware of it until the distinguished party had landed, played a round on the golf links, and returned to the steamer. It was about one o'clock when the

Enchantress, a vessel of 1,100 horse power, her white decks and cabins rising high above the water, cast anchor in the West Bay and soon afterwards the gangways were lowered and two boats were seen making for the harbour.

"On landing the visitors immediately requisitioned a couple of jaunting cars and drove to the Royal Portrush Golf Club. The Premier and First Lord (Mr. Reginald McKenna) were accompanied by Mrs McKenna, Miss Jykell, Lieutenant G. Farrie, Lieutenant Crompton, Commander H.W. Harris, Lieutenant E.T. Trowbridge and Mr. Vincent Baddelly."

On arrival at the Clubhouse, where no doubt the distinguished party must have been expected, the gentlemen entered their names in the visitors' book, and having engaged caddies (surely a red letter day for at least one of the caddies), started to play a foursome, while the ladies began a round on the ladies' course.

By now news of the VIP visit had become more widespread and notwithstanding the desire of the high profile visitors that it should be a private affair, a considerable number of holidaymakers and residents "strolled towards the links in the course of the afternoon to witness the progress of the match."

There was still an air of disbelief among a fair section of the crowd – the Prime Minister "the chief man in these realms" – playing golf in Portrush!

It was noted in another news report: "An event so interesting, one has rarely an opportunity of witnessing in these parts. Here was Mr. Asquith, throwing aside for once, the cares of State, and riveting his attention for two whole hours and a half upon the fortunes of a little white ball – this man who had been one of the most illustrious practitioners at the English bar, who by speaking seldom and well, became a man of mark in the House of Commons, and who even during the premiership of "C.B." was regarded as the real Liberal leader for all serious debating purposes."

Although much older than his opponent, the First Lord of the Admiralty, Mr. Asquith was reported to have held his own in the match, which ended in a draw.

Over the closing holes, a growing crowd of spectators had gathered to witness a little bit of history unfolding on the famous links. One sports commentator wrote: "The crowd had seen better golf. It was indeed evident that the distinguished visitors were golfers in a mild way; but no doubt in times of difficulty with the little ball, the proud reflection comes to them that they have learned to excel in something rather better than golf. A few years ago Mr. Asquith and Mr Balfour often entered into friendly rivalry on the North Berwick links. Fortunately, politics do not always interfere with the recreation of statesmen and their friendships."

Prime Minister Asquith

Afterwards, the party were rejoined by the ladies "and tea was partaken of at the Clubhouse." Both Mr. Asquith and Mr. McKenna were loud in their praise of the links course and expressed thanks to the Club Secretary, Mr. L. Stuart Anderson.

For some reason, the Prime Minister and his party decided to walk from the Clubhouse to the harbour, a comparatively short distance because in those days the clubhouse was located at Dunluce Avenue, and hence we have the Prime Minister, having slung his golf bag over his shoulders, setting off in the direction of the harbour.

At the harbour, a small crowd had gathered to witness the departure; there was some waving but no cheering and no other demonstration. Shortly after five o'clock, two small boats were rowed out from the harbour to the Enchantress and shortly afterwards she slipped away as quietly as she had arrived, "steaming away eastward."

So ended a visit which saw one of the most unlikely and unexpected games of golf to be played on the Royal Portrush links. It has no doubt been recorded somewhere in the annals of the club which, down through the years, has played host to many distinguished visitors.

But the story of the Prime Minister who walked away from the clubhouse with his bag of clubs slung over his shoulder, to board the magnificent Admiralty yacht waiting in the bay, will surely go down as one of the most intriguing.

Lining up a putt - the Prime Minister?

And here's a fascinating historical footnote: The Admiralty yacht, the Enchantress, was later to be used by Winston Churchill, when he became First Lord of the Admiralty in 1911. It became his home and office for a lengthy period and indeed, it was from this vessel that he is said to have mastered every detail of navy tactics, from gunnery to the morals of the sailors under his command.

percy french -sweeping down to the sea

On wings of fancy let me stray,
To summer shores again.

Those lines are taken from the beautiful poem, "The Island of my Dreams" by Percy French who, as an entertainer, was a regular summer visitor to Portrush and other north coast resorts in the early part of the last century. So it's possible that his flight of fancy would have brought him back to these summer shores; perhaps to the East Strand in Portrush with its stunning backdrop of the Skerries and the Causeway headlands.

The beach sketch above is copied from a painting by Percy French, one of a number of his paintings featured in the excellent book, "A Picture of Percy French" by Alan Tongue. The little girl in the painting is French's daughter, Ettie and according to the caption it was painted on a family holiday in Brittany. But I believe the painting depicts the East Strand in Portrush with the Causeway headland in the background and it may well have been painted on a family holiday in Portrush.

Undoubtedly, one of the top holiday shows in Portrush in the summers at the turn of the last century was provided by Percy French, best known, perhaps, for his famous and most endearing and enduring of songs, "The Mountains of Mourne."

His was mostly a one-man show – he was one of the few entertainers with the versatility and talent to able to hold an audience spellbound for something like two hours. Not only was he a fine singer but he was also an enthralling story-teller and a gifted artist, illustrating parts of his show with masterly and quickly executed black and white drawings.

Percy French was a fine water-colourist and I'm sure that for relaxation during the daytime he probably enjoyed nothing better than getting away to some secluded spot and setting up his easel for a painting session. Somewhere there exists, I wouldn't be surprised, a long forgotten painting or even paintings, depicting Portrush views from that time. It would be great if one was to turn up after all these years; it would be worth quite a lot of money now.

At any rate, it was as an entertainer and songwriter that the great man was best known in those days – he is described in a local Press report from that time as "one of the best known and most talented entertainers at present before the public…"

He was then at the height of his fame and his show in the Town Hall attracted capacity audiences. His extensive repertoire included the obligatory rendition of his best known composition, the "Mountains of Mourne" and it must have been a real delight to hear it sung by the composer himself. That would have been something special.

One critic who attended one of the Portrush performances wrote this: "It is notoriously difficult for one man to hold the attention of an audience for two hours on stretch; but Mr. French is endowed with the versatility which makes such an entertainment possible; and it was obvious that his hearers were interested and diverted until the very last item on the lengthy programme. Mr. French acceded to the request of his audience in rendering some of the old favourites which have made his name famous throughout the English-speaking world; the ever popular "Mountains of Mourne" was especially well received."

He must have sung that song hundreds of times in the course of concerts up and down the country so it was not too surprising that in his Portrush show he "did not trade on his reputation" but sang a selection of new numbers, all of them said to be equal in quality to his older and more widely known compositions.

For example, the song, "Flannigan's Flying Machine" was said to have been well received, with its brand of quaint, ingenious humour "of which Mr. French is a master." And quite an ambitious claim was made for another of his songs, one describing a letter written by an Irish emigrant on board an ocean liner – it bids fair, said the critic, to become as popular as its well-known prototype, the "Mountains of Mourne".

It was not only songs which made up the repertoire of his one man show. This from the same critic: "In his black-and-white sketches and colour drawings, Mr. French is as inimitable as ever. He also submitted some original verses full of point and wit and these gained much from his finished manner of recitation. The one entitled 'Later On' was a veritable tit-bit."

Mostly, the great man held court on stage for the entire show but on this occasion he departed from this custom to introduce another artiste, Mr. Harry Franklin, described as a brilliant violinist who played a number of Irish airs "with real distinction and insight."

Percy French was also a big hit when he appeared at the Picture Palace in between performances. The proprietors, announcing a forthcoming appearance, described it like this: "An event of unusual interest will take

Strolling along Main Street

102

place next week when, for the first three nights of the week, the management have pleasure in announcing that they have engaged that well-known entertainer and humorist, Mr. Percy French, who will appear in addition to the usual magnificent display of pictures.

"Mr. French is well known to Portrush audiences and is deservedly a popular favourite. He will, during this visit, introduce several new numbers, not forgetting the old favourites."

It was emphasised that the visit was for three nights only and that owing to the expense involved, the admission prices for the first three nights would be two shillings, one shilling and sixpence. Later in the week, in addition to the usual display, it was announced that "a splendid film" entitled "Captain Scott at the South Pole," would be shown "which would repay anyone a visit to the Picture Palace." The admission price for this would be the usual one shilling, sixpence and threepence.

I wonder if Mr. French ever met up with another equally famous entertainer who also made regular appearances in Portrush – the great Harry Lauder. For him, appearing at Portrush must have felt like coming home because his shows were patronised by hundreds of his fellow countrymen who flocked to the north coast resort during the various Scottish fair holidays, most of them coming over on the Ardrossan to Portrush steamship service.

The local newspaper, the Constitution, carried an interview with Mr. Lauder in June of 1913 in which he looked back on his career which had started in London some ten years earlier.

The great Harry Lauder - performing in Portrush

He recalled some of the songs he had sung on that occasion – "Tobermory", "Calligan" and "The Lass of Killiecrankie". He had very clear memories of agents, managers and proprietors buzzing around him like bees before the week was out, such was the impact he had made. "Almost before I realised that I had made good, I was signing contracts binding me hand and foot for years," he added.

Two of his favourite songs were "She's ma Daisy" and "The Saftest o' the Family" – many people had told him these were among the best things he ever did and he quite agreed with that statement. "I think they are great character songs. The American public simply insist on having them and I may yet put them on again here."

A song which was another hit for him was "Stop yer Ticklin' Jock" and he sang it until, in his own words "ma verra thrapple was sair laughin'. Interestingly, he told the Constitution that a miner from the Klondyke had told him that this song was the favourite gramophone selection in Dawson City. The same miner had travelled all the way to New York just to see him when he was performing in that city.

His most popular song, however, was probably "I Love a Lassie" which was originally heard at his first pantomime in Glasgow some seven years earlier. "I can only describe it as a terrific success both there and in London," he said.

Three years earlier he produced "We Parted on the Shore" which was undoubtedly sung on many occasions at Portrush harbour as the Scottish visitors took their leave, many bidding farewell to newly acquired friends.

Here's to Mr. French and Mr. Lauder and the fine contribution they made to tourism in Portrush in that old, golden age.

Castles in the sand.

Last port of call for an old convict ship

*The ship's crew deserted and headed
for the goldfields...*

O ne of the most unusual ships ever to drop anchor at Portrush was
an old convict ship named, rather strangely, "Success" and although
there is some doubt about this, the visit most probably took place
some time during the summer of 1912.

A tattered old poster describes the ship as "the sight of a lifetime" and it
surely must have been; no doubt it would have attracted a good deal of
curiosity and interest among visitors and residents alike. On that old poster
someone has scribbled "1904 approx." and that is the only reference there
is as to the time of the visit.

But I am fairly certain that it was much later than that and the old poster
gives a couple of clues which would tend to confirm this. For example, it
notes that the visit of the "Success" was while the ship was "en route to
America." Records show that the old ship crossed the Atlantic in 1912 and
spent the next twenty years or so touring around various ports in America.
So Portrush could well have been her last port of call before her Atlantic
crossing.

That old poster also highlighted the fact that the "Success" had been 17
years on tour as a museum ship at the time of her Portrush visit. Again, her

seafaring history states that after a thorough refit she began touring Australian ports before heading for England, arriving in Dungeness on 12 September, 1895. So by 1912, as the poster announced, she would have been 17 years on tour.

I'm sure the chance of being shown over a former convict ship would have been a huge attraction for many people, visitors and residents alike, but alas I can find no reference to the visit in the local newspapers.

The "Success" was an impressive looking vessel of 621 tons, full masted, and she had been built at Tenasserim in Burma in 1840. In May 1852 she arrived at Melbourne – most of the passengers were emigrants. It was the time of the great gold rush in Australia and the ship's crew deserted and headed for the goldfields. At this time prisons were packed to overflowing and so the Government of Victoria tried to solve the problem by purchasing large sailing ships for use as prison hulks.

When no longer needed as a prison ship, the "Success" was bought by a group of entrepreneurs and fitted out as a museum ship, the intention being that she should travel the world, putting on display "the perceived horrors of the convict era". And that is how, one day in the summer of 1912, she sailed into Portrush. How long she stayed is not known but undoubtedly her visit must have been a great attraction for the area.

One last sad note: the "Success" fell into disrepair in the late 1930s and was destroyed by fire while being dismantled for her teak on 4 July, 1946 at Cleveland, Ohio.

horse-play on the sands

- MAURICE McALEESE -

"…complaints about
  'Wild West' gallops along the beach."

One of the most enduring images of a holiday by the seaside must surely be the sight of donkeys and ponies huddled in a little group on the beach, children being helped into the saddle and holding tightly onto reins as they "steer" their mounts along by the edge of the sea.

This was certainly the case in Portrush a century ago on both the East and West Strands and mostly it was an enjoyable experience for youngsters and some adults as well. Things didn't always run smoothly, however, and sometimes serious objections were raised concerning the matter of cruelty to the animals. Complaints of this nature were debated at a meeting of the town council on foot of a letter which had been received from the Ulster Society for the Prevention of Cruelty to Animals. The Society understood, the letter stated, that the Council was taking over control of the East Strand from the Portrush end to the gasworks. It was that section on which ponies for hire were usually kept, and they had received many complaints about the ill-treatment of the animals from time to time during the past year. The Society wanted the Council to take drastic action, urging them not to grant permission for the ponies to trade on the sands during the coming season.

What the Society complained about most of all was the treatment of the ponies by "big, rough boys" who were permitted to ride them. They were not blaming the owners, their Inspectors having reported that the ponies were well cared for. Nevertheless, complaints that they were "over-ridden" had been received and the point was made that in seaside resorts in England, the use of such ponies was restricted to young people under 14 years of age. Two ladies representing the interests of the Society attended the meeting and one of them, Miss Hamilton, J.P., said the riding of ponies over soft sand was considered very cruel. She was replying to a member who said there was no doubt that the ponies provided great amusement for the children and were a great attraction.

The ladies received strong support from one of the councillors who said the riding of ponies and horses on the strand should be banned, claiming that he had nearly been knocked down on one occasion.

One of his colleagues said the practice complained of had become a formidable amusement in Portrush and one the Council would have to take notice of. He had received numerous complaints and he added: "When, as often happened, big country fellows rode the ponies it could not be denied that there was cruelty. As to the bigger horses, these were often galloped at a fearful rate and were frequently in a lather of sweat. That was not amusement; it was cruelty."

He highlighted also the danger which this posed to members of the public, expressing the view that it was a wonder that children had not been run down before now. The Strand was not now a safe place for people using it.

It was not only "big rough fellows" who were being blamed – some ladies also found themselves at the wrong end of the debate when one of the councillors said there might be some confusion between ponies and horses that were let out for riding lessons. He told the meeting: "I have seen ladies riding the latter and they are not particular whether they take the animals onto hard or soft sand."

Mr Henry Ireland
and his donkeys on
the East Strand

The Council chairman assured the ladies from the Society they were agreed that there should not be any cruelty to the animals, but they were anxious not to interfere with the legitimate pleasure of any section of their visitors. The matter, he said, would be given careful consideration.

No decision was taken at the meeting, the matter being referred to the Improvement Committee. The Committee must have come up with some kind of solution because the tradition of ponies and donkeys on the beach at Portrush, and the huge enjoyment which they gave to children particularly, continued for many years afterwards, hopefully without any more "Wild West" gallops along the beach!

street gambLing Led to a riot!

*"Eventually a number of policemen arrived on the
scene and placed four men under arrest."*

W hat may be described as street gambling was starting to become
something of a problem in Portrush a century ago and the point is
well made in an incident which occurred in the summer of 1913.

In those days it was, apparently, all too easy for anyone so inclined to set
up so-called "gambling tables" at various locations in the town, particularly
at the north end of Main Street and in the vicinity of Ramore Hill, and they
were a familiar spectacle in the holiday season. The chance of winning a
few pounds on the roulette wheel, or on the turn of a card, must have been
a big temptation for many.

One Friday evening in July of that year the spin of the wheel went all wrong
for one gambling man from Desertmartin while on an excursion visit to
Portrush. He succumbed to the lure of the roulette wheel and the outcome,
as the local Press reported, was "an altercation" with the man who was
operating the gambling table. Just what led to the altercation was not made
clear but presumably it had something to do with either the winning or
losing of a bet. Be that as it may, it was alleged that the operator of the
roulette wheel had "hit the excursionist in the face with a stick." The report
went on: "Other members of the excursion party rushed to the aid of their
comrade, whose assailant had also several backers, and a free fight ensued.

"Gambling tables were overturned, and eventually the roulette wheel
proprietor sought safety in the dwelling house of a woman named Doherty.
He was pursued by an angry mob and they smashed some of the windows
of this and an adjoining house." In the words of an eye-witness "the place
resembled a Donnybrook in miniature." Another view was that the roulette
table proprietor would have undoubtedly fared badly had he not recognised
that discretion was the better part of valour. He did not stay in Mrs Doherty's

house for too long, making his escape by the back door and getting "clean away."

Eventually a number of policemen arrived on the scene and placed four men under arrest. There was some resistance from the men and their supporters, obliging the police to draw their batons owing to the menacing attitude of the crowd. Fortunately they did not have to use the batons because some local people intervened and were able to hold the crowd in check. The arrested men were taken to the police barracks and subsequently brought before the local magistrate, Captain Watt J.P. They were later released on bail to appear before the Petty Sessions. As a result of that incident, the excursion train was delayed for about an hour.

Some weeks later the question of gambling in the town was raised at a meeting of the Urban Council when a memorial or petition extensively signed by merchants and others was discussed. The council was asked "to give directions that the thoroughfares at the north end of Main Street be kept clear of people with roulette tables and other nuisances and obstructions."

One of the council members was reported as saying it was a pity they could not pass bye-laws "to keep this rubbish out of the town altogether."

Another moved that the police be informed of the council's desire to have the streets cleared of such obstructions, and that the District Inspector should direct the members of the constabulary to take action in the matter. This was passed unanimously.

Just what action the police were able to take and what, if any, effect it had on the gambling problem is not clear but somehow I think it would not have been all that easy to deal with and the lure of the gambling tables probably remained a feature of the holiday scene in Portrush, particularly during busy periods, for a good many more years.

A year earlier, during the busiest day of the year (July 13) another report had highlighted the fact that at the Dock Head entrance to Ramore Hill "a large area of public thoroughfare, has been transformed into a veritable showground."

There was an amazing variety of attractions including roulette tables, shooting galleries, dolly mollies, peg tumbling, dart throwing, photography, height and weight telling machines, fortune reading, sweetmeat and novelty hawking, and "numerous other devices for money-making – for the proprietors, of course!"

You're probably wondering what "dolly mollies" are and I must confess I don't have a clue – perhaps there was a child's doll of that name - but it's a safe bet that they were part of the so-called money-making devices.

Yet another source of irritation in Portrush at that time was the large number of hawkers and itinerant traders who descended on the town in the busy summer months, sometimes setting up their own stalls and displaying their wares. On the crowded streets there was always someone trying to sell something to the many visitors and they could be quite persistent. Apparently there was nothing to stop them doing so but towards the end of the summer of 1913, local councillors were debating the possibility of putting a curb on their activities.

The suggestion was made that perhaps they could be confined to a designated area where they could operate in more controlled surroundings. It was something which the Council voted to consider at a future meeting but some members were sceptical about such an approach, so dealing with the problem was not straightforward and as far as I know Portrush never had a designated area for market traders.

In view of all that, two gentlemen were perhaps unfortunate to be arrested by the police for conducting unlawful games on the public roadway. The offence happened at Cloughorr on the outskirts of the town adjacent to where Hanneford's circus was encamped. No mention is made as to the nature of the unlawful games they were conducting but they were brought before the local magistrate and each was sentenced to imprisonment for a month with hard labour.

A busy scene at Lansdowne

down the chute at the blue pool

"...the fair sex grumble that they are not permitted to use it."

Aquatic displays were an important part of the holiday scene in Portrush 100 years ago and indeed for a long time afterwards, but those old displays were, by all accounts, "simply the best" - apologies to Tina Turner!

They were also billed sometimes as water carnivals and in the summer of 1911 they were at the height of their popularity, particularly at the South Pier, or harbour bathing-place. According to one source, the number of spectators attending one of these events in July of that year was so large that many people "including a number of daring young ladies" were perched on the roofs of bathing boxes, from where, no doubt, they would have had a splendid view of the proceedings.

"Quite a number of pleasure boats moved to and fro in the vicinity, and the scene was therefore, unusually animated", a reporter wrote. "The weather was delightful and this, together with the varied programme, afforded the spectators much delight."

The programme included a number of swimming races for which there was an array of prizes, including gold and silver medals, surprisingly, so the competition must have been quite intense. It was not all serious stuff, however – there was an umbrella race and just what that entailed is anybody's guess but no doubt it was highly entertaining. It is on record that "a number of other bathers joined in amusing the spectators by getting through some comic events, including the greasy pole, the barber's shop and fancy diving."

The results of some of the racing that day: 100 yards swimming race (for boys under 18 years of age) – 1, Master L. Chubb, Portrush (winner of the silver medal); 2, Master Norman Mee, Londonderry; 3, Master H.C.C. Chubb, Portrush. 100 yards swimming race (open) – 1, Mr. J. Battersea. Ladies' swimming race (open) – 1, Miss Aileen Mee, Londonderry (winner of gold medal); 2, Miss Jeannie Cummins, Coleraine. Umbrella race – 1, Mr. Bernard Munier, N.C. Hotel, Portrush.

Mr. W. H. Scott, Newry acted as starter and the judges were Messrs David Irvine and H. Perry, Londonderry.

Diving displays, or water carnivals, were also held at the Blue Pool, another popular venue with its natural amphitheatre of rocks providing good vantage points for the hundreds of spectators usually in attendance.

The emphasis, it has to be said, seems to have been more on entertainment value than expertise in diving or swimming. At one Blue Pool display in the summer of 1913 a dramatic accident and rescue was staged and it was done so realistically that many of the spectators were apparently "oblivious to the fact that it had all been arranged."

What happened involved the capsizing of a small rowing boat in which were two ladies named as "the Misses Reynolds" and it seems that "their efforts to get out of the water, and the conduct of the hero who got them safely on board again, was very exciting" so much so that many of the spectators "heaved a sigh of relief" when the ladies were finally rescued.

Again, for the record, those taking part in that display were listed as follows: Junior diving – Willie Duff, D. Service, D. McMullan and R. Telford. Miscellaneous chute – H. Gilmore, A. T. Logan, R. Telford, D. Service and W. Duff. High Diving (a) J. R. Patterson (Derry) D. Mc Mullan, T. Murray, A.T. Logan and H. Gilmore. High diving (b) – J.A. Thompson, R. Robb, S.T. Cochrane, D. Corry and E. Hamilton. Greasy pole – Cecil Black, D. Service and G. Pinion.

It is recorded also that "some special turns" were given by Mr. D.F. Scott, an English gentleman who had taken up residence in Portrush and was known far and wide as something of a character, contributing much to the local community in many spheres of endeavour. He would undoubtedly have been a familiar figure to many holidaymakers.

An indication of just how popular these diving and swimming displays were is given in a Press report of one such event in the summer of 1912. The rocks around the Blue Pool, it was stated, "presented an animated spectacle" with the attendance being estimated at between seven and eight hundred people. The display given was described as "most interesting" and a highlight had been an exhibition of graceful and fancy diving off the top rock. So there was not a diving board as such for the high divers - the rock face was about 30 feet high – and this must have added to the spectacle.

Perhaps one of the largest and most exciting water carnivals ever staged at Portrush took place in the summer of 1902 when the big attraction was an international water polo match between teams from Wales and Ireland. The Ireland team included two players from the Belfast Amateur Swimming Club, W.E. Morris and J. Carmichael.

Carmichael had the distinction of scoring the first goal for Ireland and by half time they led by two goals to nil. However, Wales had the best of play in the second half and ran out winners by four goals to three.

That was probably the one and only time an international water polo match was played in Portrush. It took place at the harbour under the auspices of the Blue Pool Amateur Swimming Club because of course the Blue Pool, a rather confined space, would not have been suitable for such an event. It's interesting to know that there was a Blue Pool Amateur Swimming Club at one time. Their members would have been pleased, no doubt, when the Urban Council decided to erect a water chute, adding still further to the amenities.

It was provided in the summer of 1912 and at the time it was believed Portrush was the only seaside resort in Ireland to have one. It came about because of pressure from a group of visitors. A memorial signed by 36 visitors who came regularly to Portrush was handed in to the Urban Council and it was considered at a subsequent meeting. The petitioners were feeling hard done by, pointing out that at the majority of fashionable watering places, chutes were erected and gave a vast amount of pleasure to visitors. The Council agreed that a chute should be installed, provided the cost did not exceed £5!

The chute was duly erected but it re-opened an old can of worms for the Council – the question of mixed bathing which was not allowed here, being the preserve of male bathers. However, the ladies felt that they were being deprived of a lot of fun, not being able to take advantage of this great new facility, and there were even more rumblings than before. Ladies had their own bathing place at Murtagh's Mouth, not all that far from the Blue Pool, but it was not so well appointed, so perhaps it was not too surprising when it was reported that one young lady had popped over and enjoyed a "header" down the chute, something which probably happened quite a lot in spite of the ban.

There was, perhaps, a glimmer of hope on the horizon for the deprived ladies. The installation of the chute, seen as such a great attraction, may have signalled the end of the "male only" bathing rule at the Blue Pool. There is certainly a hint of this in this news item: "The fair sex grumble that they are not permitted to use it, and think it unreasonable that mixed bathing should be prohibited here, and allowed at the harbour. This is a matter for the municipal authorities. Perhaps if another memorial was forwarded to the Council, signed by those interested, the request might be acceded to. The ladies certainly have a grievance."

However, the town council was not always easily persuaded to make changes and improvements, even in response to complaints from members of the public. In July, 1903 the editor of The Constitution published a long letter from a contributor using the pseudonym "Amphibious" complaining about the neglected state of the Blue Pool. He wrote: "I do not hesitate to say that the Blue Pool has brought many a thousand pounds to Portrush. Why then is it so neglected? The principal bathing box is in sad need of attention. The floor is as undulating as the waters of the pool, and its motion is far from musical. It groans at every footstep, and loudly reproaches the authorities for their neglect of it.

"A broken window of considerable standing is unnecessary for ventilation, insufficient for purposes of view, and fails to disclose to prying outsiders more than a very limited position of the manly form of the bathers within. It is innocent of paint – a cheap commodity which the stalwart and obliging attendant might occupy his leisure in applying to its weather-beaten boards."

This correspondent could obviously use humorous turns of phrase to telling advantage in pressing home his various points. He continued: "The concrete steps leading from the box to the pool are on an inclined plane and have so smooth a surface that when they are wet they form a dangerous trap, and cases are of frequent occurrence where bathers find their scanty and attenuated costumes a poor protection when they come in sudden contact with them."

He suggested a solution to the problem: "A little roughening with a chisel would be a comfort, and save many a black and blue design on a variety of parts of the human frame and many an abraded shin. It is surely not too much to ask that this state of matters might be improved. It does not require an Act of Parliament nor an order of the Local Government Board. A pot or two of paint, a sheet of glass less than a square foot, a few nails, and a few hours' work of a tradesman would transform the place at the expense of a few shillings."

A week or so later the letter was mentioned at a meeting of the Urban Council and it was not well received. One member said that if the facts in the letter were true then the improvements suggested should be carried out. He had been speaking to the attendant who had stated that the floors of the bathing huts were bad and required work to be done to them. He moved that the improvements should be carried out.

The Clerk, however, intervened to say that he considered the arrangements of the Blue Pool "very satisfactory." The huts were in a good condition and the improvements were not necessary. Accordingly, no action was taken in the matter.

Obviously there was no fear of litigation in those days resulting from personal injury and it would be interesting to know just how the health and safety regulations were implemented and how the Clerk, in this instance, reached the conclusion that no action required to be taken.

BLUE POOL PORTRUSH Co ANTRIM 2217.W.L

shifting winds and changing tides

"With a slack west tide, and the net set wide,
It's the silv'ry salmon we follow."

T he lot of the North Coast fishermen was not an easy one a century ago but in Portrush they were fortunate enough to be able to augment their income in the summer time by operating pleasure craft in and around the harbour and out to the Skerry Islands.

The harbour had a magnetic appeal for tourists; diving displays and water carnivals drew huge crowds and there were always plenty of people on the quayside eager to watch the arrival and departure of the cross-Channel steamers. The small fleet of fishing boats attracted a good deal of interest, too, particularly when catches were being unloaded.

In the summer of 1913 the fishermen of Portrush were experiencing one of their worst ever seasons – according to one newspaper report, it was the worst for years. The catches being landed at Portrush, Portstewart and around the coast as far as Ballintoy were described as "exceedingly poor."

In a newspaper interview, one old Portrush resident who lived close to the harbour, remembered those old days and recalled the hard life and times the fishermen had to overcome in trying to earn a living from the sea. "Their's was a hard lot," he said. "The return for the hazardous toil was meagre and when, through stress of wind and tide, they could not pursue their calling on the deep, their families were frequently in dire distress."

He was speaking of a time well before the advent of the motor trawler. "Not infrequently," he went on "through shifting winds, the men had to row their boats eight or ten miles to and from the fishing grounds and would arrive at the harbour drenched to the skin. They were brave men. In their little drontheims they battled against the elements with their long oars or their little triangle of sail. Their frail boats are no more; with few exceptions they have passed on, the boats of the hardy seamen who laid the foundations of one of the loveliest seaside places in Britain."

Although not referring specifically to the fishermen of Portrush, the unnamed writer of an article published in a nautical journal from the 1930s, also gave a glimpse of those old seafaring days at the turn of the century: "Picture them caught by the storm, their boats battered, swept, half-filled, but kept afloat by the strong arms that wielded – what? A tin dish for bailing – not even a bucket, just a dish. That, as it fell from numbed hands, was taken up by another of the drenched crew. Four men in a cockleshell defying the ocean, setting the hurricane at bay, rising triumphant against the lash of the waves, nearly beaten, yet fighting on and winning through."

...the men had to row their boats eight or ten miles to and from the fishing grounds and would arrive at the harbour drenched to the skin. They were brave men.

It was not all gloom and doom for the fishermen that summer, hard pressed though they were. It was reported that drift-net fishing for salmon on the North Antrim coast had been fairly successful. Although no very large catches were made, the weather conditions had proved more favourable than for many years and the fishermen had earned a fair livelihood. In spite of the hazardous nature of their occupation, they were described as "a cheery body of men."

Drift-net fishing often entailed fierce battles with the elements. Their hard life and times is captured in this old account of their calling: "Around our coasts during part of June and July, when the salmon are coming in from the ocean on their way to the rivers to spawn, a hardy and daring body of fishermen pursue a dangerous calling, venturing out to sea in shallops every suitable night to set their drift-nets." Ironically, it was on rough nights that the fishermen had the best chance of landing a good catch: "The coarser the night, the more successful the fishing."

Just how the boats were crewed and managed is very well described: "Four men constitute the boat's crew, and in the evenings, from 24th June to 12th July, as the sun has sunk below the horizon and dusk is falling, from little ports and bays you may see the boats steal out to sea, rowed by four pairs of sinewy arms. Out about two or three miles from the shore, where the tide turns true, the net is shot across the tide, the boat hanging on to one end, and the crew keeping an eye for passing steamers which may swoop down in the darkness and run them down or cut their net adrift. Thus they ride out the night, with perhaps a north-wester blowing half a gale, occasionally running along to see if the net is 'fishing straight' or hauling in if it runs foul, until the dawn warns that it is time to make for port."

What happened to the catch? The fish were sent for sale to local markets – during the short drift-net season the prices were low so at this time of year freshly caught salmon would be high on the menu of nearly all the hotels and guest-houses in Portrush and other north coast resorts.

One of the crew members of the north coast fishing boat, "Polly" wrote a poem about their exploits. It's quite a long poem so I'm giving just the first and last verses here:

She's as tidy a yawl, twenty-five over all,
As sails the Atlantic wave,
With a crew so bold, five men all told,
Fishermen hardy and brave,
Then it's yo, heave ho, it's goin' to blow
O'er the crest o' the wave an' the hollow,
With a slack west tide, an' the net set wide,
It's the silv'ry salmon we follow.

At the dawn o' day, when the east is grey,
We'll board at the end o' the tide,
An' shinin' bright in the mornin' light,
As the net comes over the side.
With a yo, heave ho, how meshed fish show
On the crest o' the wave an' the hollow;
Three score an' more we'll bring ashore
O' the silv'ry salmon we follow.

They were indeed "hardy and brave," those old fishermen – down through the years many also served as lifeboatmen – and I sometimes think what a pity it is that there is not some kind of memorial to them, perhaps in the shape of a bronze sculpture, at or near the harbour, to commemorate their heroic struggles and to mark the contribution they made to enhance the proud seafaring tradition which Portrush undoubtedly has.

As a young lad growing up in Portrush in the 1940s and 50s I remember seeing groups of the old fishermen, most of them in sombre navy pullovers and cloth caps, gathering at the small stone wall overlooking the harbour, surveying the scene below, and doubtless reminiscing for a good part of the time on days gone by. I'm thinking now that probably they would have had first hand experience of fishing from those old drontheims and would have battled against many a stormy sea in their quest for the silvery salmon. Years later I wrote a poem about them. It's called:

The Harbour Wall

Down by the harbour wall
The old men sit and dream,
And sea-stained stones
Their secrets seal
As on memory's tides
They sail away to old,
Familiar, foreign ports,
Leaving their poor, shackled
Horizons far behind.

Down by the harbour wall
The old ships pull and strain,
And barnacle-encrusted
Moorings hold fast their
Noble, creaking hulls,
Washed by missed tides,
As they catch night's Crescent
In the black, beckoning depths.

- MAURICE McALEESE -

the street entertainers

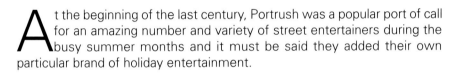

*"There was also a blind fiddler...who
played while his aged mother sang, in
a quavering voice, "Sweet Vale of Avoca."*

A t the beginning of the last century, Portrush was a popular port of call
for an amazing number and variety of street entertainers during the
busy summer months and it must be said they added their own
particular brand of holiday entertainment.

One of the more unusual street entertainers in the North Antrim area at that
time was a man with a very novel act – his speciality was throwing turnips
into the air and breaking them on his head as they fell!

Not surprisingly, perhaps, his headline act always drew a large audience. I
wonder if he wore any kind of protective headgear while performing this
amazing feat – if not he must surely have suffered quite a few headaches
from one performance to the next! Hopefully, the turnips were not wasted
and were recycled in some way.

In those days the travelling troubadours would make regular appearances
all over Ireland and the length of time they stopped over in any town or
village would be determined by the level of patronage achieved. One of the
most popular shows was provided by a gentleman called Dan Fields whose
show was slightly more sophisticated in that it took place in a wooden booth
covered by a canvas roof.

This description is culled from an old newspaper report: "The wooden
portion of the booth was constructed in sections to admit of its being taken

down and packed on carts to facilitate its transit from town to town. There was a raised wooden dancing platform in front of the structure on which the various performers gave an open-aid demonstration of their diverse talents preliminary to the show proper inside."

Usually a violinist, cornet player and big drummer "discoursed" the music. Dan himself, wonderfully made up and clad in sundry hairy skins of animals, and carrying clanking chains, was led by a keeper and exhibited through the streets as The Wild Man of the Woods each evening before the show commenced. Just what sort of performance was given by the wild man of the woods was not revealed in that old account but no doubt it went down a treat with patrons, especially the youngsters.

Another entertainer who was a regular was Johnnie Bolton, who owned a variety show. He possessed "a wonderful ancient brass musical instrument" and even though it was black with age and tarnished and battered with much travel and use, he played sweet music on it.

The report noted: "It was much larger than a cornet, and even then it must have been a relic of a bygone age. Johnnie was accompanied by his wife, to whom he showed great deference. She was a little old lame lady, an infirmity which it was supposed she received when jumping out of a window of her father's house to elope with the strolling actor."

The arrival in town of a travelling company of actors was sometimes announced in "stentorian" tones during a procession through the streets to whip up interest and one example of this is given in relation to the McCormick Stock Company, whose leading actor was called Johnnie Dick, described as a tragedian.

While beating a big drum, Johnnie's booming voice proclaimed: "The public are most respectfully informed that the theatre is now open, commencing with a very much admired drama entitled 'Gilroy, the Hero of Scotland' to be followed afterwards with a variety of singing and dancing, the whole to wind up with a laughable farce entitled 'Jennie, put the kettle on'."

After the announcement the band would strike up and the procession would move on to the next corner where it would be repeated once more. Incidentally, the admission charge was one penny to the gallery and twopence to the pit.

The circus also visited on a regular basis, in those days Bell's Circus was one of the most popular and the visit was described as a red letter day for the town. In the same category was Wombell's Menagerie, with its elephants and dromedaries, and Tommy Todd, the midget, and the strong man who enters the lion's den – people would flock from far and wide to see this performance.

There were other less daring acts which nevertheless attracted a great deal of interest. One of these was provided by a street juggler whose speciality was spinning plates on top of a stick, balanced on a pipe, which in turn was balanced on his nose. There was also a blind fiddler who played while his aged mother sang, in a soft, quavering voice, "Sweet Vale of Avoca." Another man played a fiddle improvised from a beef tin and yet another played the bagpipes while at the same time carrying a big drum on his back which he beat with a drumstick strapped to his elbow.

The old time street entertainers were very ingenious in devising instruments with which to captivate an audience. One of them, a man called John King, had made a weird and wonderful instrument from pieces of brass and tin strung on a shillelagh. It must have made a fantastic sound and I like the name he invented for his unusual instrument – he called it his 'shequinahag.'

Seafront shows were a big attraction.

In the summer of 1909, Main Street in Portrush was described in a local news report as being "fair-like" and the writer went on to give this illuminating observation of the old entertainers at work: "A tattered female figure was extolling the merits of certain ballads; the street artist was busy with his crayons; a cartful of ripe bananas was offered for sale; and over all the din was heard a street preacher, with the bell-man hard by industriously warning the crowd of the approaching tram. Farther along the street a thick circle of noisy spectators surrounded a little crow-like man whose feet were tapping a square board to the strains of a melodeon, and who also rang a bell, but an electro-plated one, as he dance. This was 'Erchie' the familiar vocalist from across the water, who is often seen on the kerbstone giving voice to 'The Lass of Killiemacrankie' and other popular airs of his native land. Erchie may be, and frequently is, provokingly chafed and teased by his countrymen on holiday, yet he never gets 'the hump' and they sometimes oblige him by passing round his silk hat, nothing the worse for wear, and returning it heavy with silver, the jingle of which brings a smile to Erchie's good natured face."

Even in those days the street entertainers were beginning to pass into history – they belong, as one commentator noted, to a declining order, although ballad singers were still to be found on every road in Ireland. And he added this nice tribute to the travelling troubadours:

"They are companionable men. Their way of livelihood brings them into pleasant relations with the world and consequently they are more amiable than tramps, tinkers, race-card vendors or roulette practitioners; they have not taken to the roads because of any artistry in their natures, and consequently they have none of the reticence of men with the gift – pipers, fiddlers and the like; they are moreover genuine idlers, and as such fond of company."

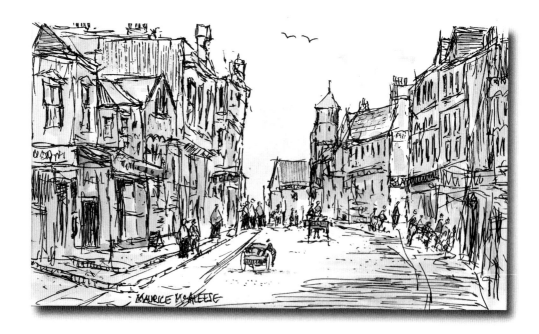

sitting "familiar" on the old jaunting cars

"Finally, the Council decided to fix the speed limit at five miles per hour."

N ever were so many motor-cars seen in the locality and, let us add, never did such clouds of dust envelop and darken the roads...

That observation on the joys of motoring in Portrush in the early part of the twentieth century is taken from a local news report published in 1910. Apart from motor-cars, licensed jaunting cars were also having "a royal time." Here is a humorous little anecdote from the period concerning the seating arrangements on the old jaunting-cars:

"How many does the car seat" asked the old lady. "Well, ma'am, if you wish to sit adjacent it seats four, but if you sit familiar, it seats six!" It has been observed, it was noted, that visitors from the West of Scotland invariably preferred to sit familiar, especially if they happened to be a mixed party.

On the subject of familiar seating, it is recorded that on one evening a procession of no fewer than twelve jaunting-cars had arrived from Portstewart, each one "laden to the peril of its springs." On these occasions it was not, apparently, a question of how many the car can seat, or the poor horse can draw, but how many can somehow be packed on the seats – and between them!

On another occasion a confrontation between an old jarvey and a youth had a sequel in court when the youth was charged with assault. It appears that the young man took the jarvey's whip and refused to give it back, striking out at the old man with it. He ran off but was later apprehended by police and the following day was brought before the local magistrate. He tried to palm off the whole incident as a practical joke but the court did not accept his version of events and he was fined two shillings and sixpence and ordered to pay the same amount in compensation to the jarvey.

The question of the suitability of the roads to contend with this increased volume of traffic was being raised, and it was argued that because of the increased volume of traffic, the quality of the roads was being severely tested. There were many pot-holes particularly on the coast road between Portrush and Portstewart, a road which, from the scenic standpoint, was regarded as one of the finest in the district, but as a thoroughfare was now, it was claimed, one of the worst.

Just a few years later, careless and sometimes reckless driving was becoming something of a problem in Portrush. In the summer of 1913 concern was being voiced more and more frequently about the behaviour of some motorists and their apparent disregard for road safety.

The problem that particular summer, according to one source, was that there had been an unprecedented eruption of motors of every kind. Now, for the first time, the spotlight was being placed fairly and squarely on motorists and motor-cyclists and the manner of their driving.

This is how the matter was highlighted in The Constitution: "Motor-cars and motor-cycles are to be seen on all the roads, followed by trails of suspended dust. Their presence indicates prosperity and enterprise, and no one would have anything but praise for them if they would but approach and pass through towns and villages at a reasonable rate of speed."

The paper did not pull any punches, offering this explanation for such behaviour: "Many of them seem to pride themselves in defying laws and regulations. They have no sort of regard for speed limit. Undoubtedly the worst offenders are motor-cyclists, the riders of which show increasing recklessness. Dozens of them rush into and out of Portrush every day. Forty miles an hour would not be too high an estimate to give to the rate of speed at which these usually noisy machines are driven..."

Inevitably, attention was drawn to the dangers which this posed to pedestrians and other road users. There had been not a few close shaves, especially at dangerous corners in the town.The police, apparently, took a laid back view of the errant motorists – it was claimed they never interfered. With some frustration, the editorial writer concluded: "Not, we suppose,

till a serious accident occurs, will the reckless and inconsiderate motorists be put down."

However, a clampdown was about to be put on the speeding motorists by the town council following a debate in which the seriousness of the problem was highlighted. It was the Council's Sanitary and Improvement Committee which reported having considered a letter from Antrim County Council stating that the speed limit for motorists in the county was 20 miles per hour, and this applied to urban districts as well as to rural districts, with the exception of Carrickfergus urban district.

In this case the speed limit had been reduced to ten miles per hour. The Committee reported that "as the urban district of Portrush consists of streets almost entirely used as promenades in the summer time, and were in consequence generally in a congested state, and as the district was not one through which motorists had to pass going to other places, it being the terminus, it was recommended that the Council should take the necessary steps to have a bye-law made that the limit in speed in the district should not exceed five miles an hour."

Even in those days, five miles an hour might have seemed a little draconian but surprisingly, some of the councillors felt that the speed limit should be reduced still further, advocating just four miles per hour. One of them commented that while he did not like to see motorists speeding, he felt that a five miles per hour limit was a walking pace. He suggested that the limit should be set at eight miles per hour. Yet another councillor made this interesting ecclesiastical point: "I would like to see the motorists going past churches at a slower speed on Sundays as they can be heard distinctly while services are in progress."

The Clerk of the Council sounded a warning. He said that if they fixed the speed limit at five miles per hour, motorists would take advantage of that and drive through the streets at that rate. He thought five miles per hour would be an alarming speed at which to drive through Portrush in the summer season.

During the debate it was pointed out also that if they limited motorists to five miles per hour, they would have to do the same with regard to bread-vans and hackney-car drivers who often exceeded that limit. Finally, the Council decided to adopt the committee recommendation fixing the speed limit at five miles per hour.

Rather oddly, none of the councillors questioned just how the speed limit would be enforced. Even in those early days of motoring, adhering to a speed limit of just five miles per hour would be something of a real test. What kind of detection, if any, would be put in place? Perhaps the Council felt that was a matter for the local constabulary.

He explained that for the coming season they were procuring an extra horse.

Accidents, whether due to speed or not, did happen. In the same issue of the newspaper, it was reported that a little girl had had a narrow escape from being knocked down by a motorist in Eglinton Street. She had stepped off the footpath into the path of an oncoming car. Her life was probably saved by another pedestrian who shouted a warning to the child and she managed to jump clear in time.

The same day there had been a fatal accident – fortunately it did not involve a human life but that of a little Pomeranian dog belonging to a visitor. It was struck by a car in Causeway Street.

Earlier in the same week, there had been a traffic accident in the town centre when an English lady tourist was knocked down in Eglinton Street.

She had just alighted from the Causeway tram when two motorists endeavoured to pass. The lady was struck by one of the cars and knocked to the ground. It was yet another lucky escape, however, because apart from shock, she was unhurt.

A familiar sight on the streets of Portrush in those days was the water-cart, a horse-drawn water wagon, which sprayed large quantities of water to keep down dust and blowing sand, a nuisance to pedestrians and a hazard to motorists. At a meeting of the town council in April, 1903 a councillor complained about the manner in which the streets of the town had been watered the previous summer. He said the work had started about two o'clock in the afternoon and had caused great discomfort to visitors.

The Town Surveyor, in reply, did not acknowledge the discomfort of visitors but explained that for the coming season they were procuring an extra horse for watering purposes and probably the provision of a chain pump for extracting sea water more expeditiously than at present. He added: "The steam-rolling and bottoming of several of the streets has added immensely to their appearance, and in a town where the blown sea sand is so common, the purchase of an additional watering-cart is an urgent necessity."

Obviously, in those early days of motoring, the whole question of road safety was coming more into the spotlight and it is interesting to note the distinctions which were being made with regard to the introduction of speed limits in town and country.

Sunshine and shadows in Main Street

boat building history

*"There is not another sailing bay in
the North of Ireland as that which
lies between The Skerries and the mainland."*

A little bit of boat-building history was recorded in Portrush in 1911 when the first motor-driven fishing boat to be built in the town was launched. Some north coast fishermen had already "jumped ship" and were embracing "the new order of things," as one nautical writer put it. So the Portrush launch was a significant event and it signalled the beginning of a prosperous new era for the local boat-building industry – and an easier life, hopefully, for the fishermen.

"There is a strong possibility that an increasingly important industry will soon be firmly established," was the confident prediction made in one news report, which added: "For utilitarian purposes the superiority of the motor-boat over the ordinary type of sailing craft is as assured as the triumph of the taxi over the horse-cab."

Portrush already had a proud tradition in the building of boats – for decades it had been one of the leading centres for the building of drontheims, also known as yawls. Moville, just across the bay, was another centre for the building of these boats. They were exported mostly to Scotland where they were known as skiffs.

At the turn of the last century, there were several boat-builders in Portrush and the output was mainly yachts and fishing craft. One of the leading boat-builders was James Kelly, described as "the famous boat-builder" and his boatyard was just off Causeway Street, overlooking the East Strand. It was a prominent seafront location so it was something of an attraction for tourists who were able to peer into the boatyard on passing and watch some of the construction work in progress. The launch of a newly constructed boat also aroused a good deal of interest.

Mr. Kelly was also a leading figure in the civic life of the community; he was a member of the Urban Council and had been chairman for a number of years. He not only built boats but also designed them and the motor-boat that had been launched that day was fitted with steering mechanism which had been engineered to his own specifications.

A report of the launching ceremony stated: "Mr. James Kelly, U.D.C., Causeway Street, whose reputation in all branches of boat-building is so well-known, has just launched a motor fishing boat which is a model of her class."

It was a fairly substantial vessel, 46 feet long and a beam of 12 feet 6 inches, an engine room measuring 9 feet by 10 feet and a cabin of roughly the same measurements. The engine supplying the motive power was a 22 h.p. Gardner petroleum with controls to operate it fitted on deck.

This is the technical description of the steering: "The boat is steered by a wheel and screw arrangement and this is provided with double capstans driven by the engine. The idea for the steering and the capstans originated with Mr. Kelly and the work was successfully carried out by Messrs Kennedy and Son, Coleraine Foundry."

A number of other boats were under construction at the Causeway Street premises, including a mahogany launch 30 foot long and having a beam of

6 foot 6 inches. It was being built for a French customer. Again, this vessel was designed by Mr. Kelly. It was fitted with a Renault engine "of the highest class" and was completely protected from sea and rain. The controls and steering wheel had been placed side by side so that they could be easily managed by one person.

Another order which the Kelly boatyard was working on at the time was one from the Marquis of Lansdowne for use on the Kenmare River. This craft was also 30 feet long with a beam of 6 foot 9 inches and was said to be of "a very handsome design."

It was a boom time for the Kelly boat-builders because they were also building a boat intended for passenger and fishing purposes. Interestingly, the exhaust had been fitted so that it discharged through the bottom of the boat, thereby doing away with the high level of noise experienced with motor engines.

And the firm had commissions from two "gentlemen," one local and the other from Belfast. One was for a cruising boat 20 feet long and the other for a small motor dinghy. With a full order book for the new motor-boats, together with the usual sail and rowing craft, there was enough work to keep the Causeway Street yard busy for a considerable time.

In the summer of 1903 a newly constructed racing yacht named "Garavogue" was launched and formally named – the expression used in a news item is "christened" – at a ceremony at the harbour and it was watched by a large crowd of residents and visitors. The yacht, one of a new design in the 21-foot class, was described as "gracefully designed and finished in the best style of workmanship." It had been built for a member of the Dublin Bay Sailing Club, a Mr. Richardson. Mr. Richardson had been staying in Portrush for the previous few days superintending the rigging of his new yacht. In a brief address, he referred to an old custom or tradition which in olden times involved "the shedding of human blood" when a boat was being launched and contrasted this with "the happy change of modern days which substituted a bottle of wine for the blood." The "christening" ceremony was duly performed by a Portrush lady, Miss Bessie Grove who had "kindly consented to break a bottle of wine in the customary way over the yacht's bows." The yacht was successfully launched into the harbour.

The reputation which Mr. Kelly enjoyed as a boat-builder may be judged by the fact that of only five boats of the 21- foot class being built for the Dublin Bay Sailing Club, his yard was building two of them. Mr. Richardson expressed the hope that as races were being held throughout the season, Portrush people would take an interest in them as they would have two Portrush-built boats competing against three Dublin boats – he had every confidence that the Portrush boats would worthily uphold their reputation.

At about the same time, it was also reported that another well-known yachtsman, Mr. G.H. Moore-Browne, who was staying at the Northern Counties Hotel, had been cruising round the coast in his trim yacht. These two yachting stalwarts had inspired a reporter to write: "There is some talk of a regatta, and those at the head of affairs would do well to invoke the aid of these two capable yachtsmen if it is to be the success it ought to be. There is not such another sailing bay in the North of Ireland as that which lies between The Skerries and the mainland, and it is a pity that advantage should not be taken of it in this respect."

The racing yacht *Garavogue* about to be launched.

bathing costumes dilemma

*"....he suggested that a charge of one penny
should be made for drawers and two-pence
for full costume."*

In the early part of the last century, a new and "daring" trend in swimwear
was taking hold and although swimsuits for both men and women were
becoming lighter and briefer, the age of the bikini for women and short
trunks for men was still a long way off.

The question of swimwear, what was considered suitable and what was
not, was something which was being given an airing in Portrush, with its
crowded beaches and bathing places. The resort had, by order of the town
council, certain designated bathing places, mixed bathing being permitted
at only one, the South Pier at the harbour.

For whatever reason, the town council felt that it was necessary to
reinforce or re-emphasise the rule concerning the type of swimwear that
was allowed – perhaps standards had been slipping and bathers were
becoming a little more daring in the choice of costumes.

It was a matter of some concern, particularly for the bathing attendant at
the harbour, a gentleman named John McAlister – he felt so strongly about
it that he wrote a letter to the council setting out his views and suggesting
how the problem might be resolved.

In the letter he stated that he understood notices were to be posted in
connection with the public-bathing places prohibiting the use of any

costume by bathers, except long-length costumes. He begged to point out that if this rule was enforced it would result in a serious pecuniary loss to himself and the other attendants. He requested the Council to "kindly amend" the rule so that the attendants would have liberty and power to decide whether the costumes brought by bathers were sufficient or insufficient, decent or indecent. And with an eye on the financial situation, he suggested that a charge of one penny should be made for drawers and two-pence for full costume.

When the letter was read out, the Town Clerk explained that the notice referred to required gentlemen to wear neck to knee costumes. He made no mention of the ladies and what they should be wearing.

There was no debate about the matter, at least none that was reported in the Press, the Council simply instructing the Clerk to inform the attendant that they could not depart from the Bathing Committee's recommendations.

On the raft at the harbour.

Reading between the lines, one might conclude that Mr McAlister and the other attendants had been exercising a little bit of leeway with regard to the suitability or otherwise of bathing costumes – i.e. the reference to the possibility of "serious pecuniary loss" if the notice was posted.

Earlier in the meeting, the Council had considered another letter from Mr. McAlister pointing out that because of the weather, bathing during the month of June had been a complete failure.

"Up to the present," he wrote, "I have not earned more than eight-pence or nine-pence per day. Under these circumstances I would respectfully beg that you would give me a reduction on the amount of my tender; or, as an alternative, permission to make a charge of 2d per person for the use of the boxes." His plea fell on deaf ears, the Council simply marking the letter "read."

At the same meeting, the Council had considered another communication about bathing, this time from the Blue Pool attendant, Charles McAlister (perhaps a relative of John). He wrote complaining about the general condition of the Blue Pool bathing-place, which was undergoing repairs, and stating that there were no signs of the work being completed. He thought it was too bad that he was walking about doing nothing while other attendants were earning money from the 1st of June. He wanted to know what the Council was going to do about it.

One councillor thought it was a pity that the attendant had to pay a high fee for the lease of the place and that the bathing boxes should be locked up for practically a month. His opinion was that he could take proceedings against the Council for not having the boxes finished on time.

However, some of his colleagues expressed the view that it would not be wise for the Council to reduce the price of the contract made with McAlister. The weather had been so rough during the month of June that even the boxes had been ready no bathing worth mentioning would have taken place. It was decided that no action should be taken.

Later that summer, the subject of bathing was again on the Council's agenda, emanating this time from the bathers themselves and their grievance was the lack of adequate bathing box accommodation at the harbour.

West Strand and the Harbour.

A memorial signed by a large number of bathers stated: "There are not nearly enough boxes to meet the demands of the bathers, with the result that those at present in use are often uncomfortably crowded, thus causing long waiting and delay on the part of those who don't wish to go into the vitiated air of the boxes which are in many cases badly ventilated."

Rather surprisingly, it was claimed that "no distinction seems to be made between the boxes reserved for the ladies and those for the gentlemen."

Neither was there sufficient seating accommodation nor sufficient hooks for clothes in some of the boxes.

The disgruntled bathers suggested a five-point plan to remedy the situation – (1) that at least half-a-dozen commodious boxes should be erected; (2) that a door should be placed in each end of a box, with a spring lock and bolt; (3) that a hinged window should be placed above the door; (4) that the boxes should have seating accommodation down each side, with an ample supply of pegs for clothes; (5) that a certain number of boxes should be reserved for ladies and that the word 'ladies' should be painted conspicuously on them.

The only female member of the Council, Miss Hamilton, said "some little attention" should be given to a memorial like that and she suggested there were some small matters which they could attend to right away such as the provision of hooks and the matter of ventilation.

Another councillor suggested that some of the boxes were in such poor condition that they should be taken down altogether.

The general feeling was that the matter should be taken seriously and that the general public should be assured that although it was not possible to carry out major work for the present season, this would be done in time for next season.

One Councillor said it was certainly time something was done as some of the boxes had been there when he was serving his apprenticeship to the boat building 30 years ago.

A committee was appointed with a view to having the boxes inspected and having minor improvements carried out in the meantime.

In the summer of 1904 the general consensus seems to have been that bathing in Portrush had never been so widely indulged in. One of the reasons for this, it was felt, was that the Urban Council "had improved the unequalled bathing facilities which Nature had provided and put competent men in charge of the different places, the health-improving pastime has become more popular than ever it was, and as safety can always be assured at any stage of the tide, some of the bathing-places are always certain to be fully occupied. Mixed bathing is becoming more general than heretofore."

The previous summer, a group of disgruntled bathers (including two clergymen) sent a petition to the Council calling for a springboard to be erected at the harbour and complaining about a lack of accommodation for those who wanted to learn to dive. They wanted the Council to erect a springboard at the end of the south pier where the water was always of sufficient depth. This would also entail provision of a series of wooden steps at different heights suitable for those who wished to dive. Provision of these amenities, it was claimed, would cost only a few pounds and would add greatly to the pleasure of, and give great satisfaction to, "the undersigned and all other bathers who frequent the harbour."

Alas, the plea fell on deaf ears, the chairman commenting that "we have spent all our money, and we have no money to do this." No action was taken.

It would appear that in those old days a train which ran from Coleraine to Portrush at an early hour in the morning during the summer months, was used by many people who had become accustomed to taking an early morning dip. A news item from June, 1903 reported: "The bathing-places are now thoroughly equipped with comfortable bathing boxes and reliable attendants. The dippers so far have not been numerous, and the early bathing train from Coleraine is not so well patronised as it might be."

On the same subject, under the headline "An Unfair Practice" it was reported that there had been complaints that many Coleraine bathers who enjoyed an early morning dip outside the harbour (which was unattended) used the beach and rocks as dressing places; they did not use the bathing boxes for which a modest fee was charged. "It is all very well," the report continued, "to economise in pennies, but if an accident occurred the South Pier attendants would doubtless be the first called on to render aid. Their interests, therefore, merit consideration by people who will persist in bathing where there is always an element of danger."

An old time view of Portrush harbour

Links with Famous Golfers

"...in addition to great brilliance, his play was marked by marvellous consistency."

E veryone who has studied the history of Irish golf is forced to the conclusion that the prosperity which Portrush has attained in recent years is, in a very sensible measure, due to the attractions which the Golf Club has provided for visitors since its establishment...

Those words are taken from an editorial in *The Constitution* in June, 1907, a time when the game of golf was being indulged in by more and more people. The Royal Portrush links course, even then, was acknowledged to be one of the best in the Kingdom and for many visitors the lure of its well manicured fairways was irresistible. As the editorial writer went on to highlight, many championships had been played on the course in recent years, something of which the Club was justly proud.

The reason for the editorial in the first place was due to the fact that the Club, "with a view to providing better facilities for members and visitors", wanted to provide another course. At that time Club officials were trying to negotiate a new lease with the landlord, Lord Antrim, but apparently they could not see "eye to eye" over the price.

In the meantime, the Club Council had passed a resolution in favour of developing 14 new holes on ground that had been lately acquired (and presumably not belonging to Lord Antrim) stretching to the White Rocks.

In the words of the resolution "these 14 holes to be arranged so as to work in along with the present four holes outside Lord Antrim's property." A neat move – sounds as if the Club had Lord Antrim well over a barrel!

"If negotiations with the Earl of Antrim conclude satisfactorily, there is a bright future in store for the Royal Portrush Club," the editorial predicted. That prediction did come true and just over four decades later the Royal Portrush Club reached a pinnacle with the staging of the British Open Championship over the famous Dunluce links in 1951. It was won by Max Faulkner from England, a very stylish player both in technique and dress. One of the competitors on that occasion was the great Fred Daly who had won the title, four years earlier, in 1947, still the only Ulsterman to do so and, of course, a native of Portrush.

One of the most distinguished members of Royal Portrush at the turn of the last century was Dr. Anthony Traill, Provost of Trinity College, Dublin and brother of William Acheson Traill, of Causeway tram fame. Evidently Dr. Traill cut quite a dash on the golf course with, as noted by a correspondent of the time, "his wide flannel trousers and aggressive looking boots, hurriedly pursuing his ball."

The same correspondent went on to tell an amusing story as to how the great man came to take up the game in the first place. One day he was standing outside the tramway depot in Portrush, waiting for a tram, when his attention was drawn to two aspiring golfers who were said to be "making desperate but ineffectual efforts to drive the famous Crater Bunker."

After watching them for a while Dr. Traill "who does not suffer from shyness" went over to them and told them what he thought of their efforts. He was immediately challenged to have a go himself if he thought he could do any better. The story goes: "At the first attempt the Dr. landed the ball on the green and departed in triumph," presumably leaving the two beginners scratching their heads in amazement. Dr. Traill went on to become a very competent player and at the time when this little anecdote was being recalled (in March, 1903) he was reckoned to be "at his age" the best player in Ireland.

From time to time a golf correspondent would be tipped off about some unusual incident which had occurred on the links and these were faithfully reported. This is how one such incident was recorded:

"Golfers, more especially golfers not quite up to championship level, are occasionally surprised by the vagaries of the ball in its flight from the tee.

The other day a player on the first tee at Portrush made a fine, strong swipe with his driver and the ball, swerving slightly to the right, struck one of the wire stays of the flagpole and rebounded back past the Clubhouse with such vigour that its wild career was only terminated by the long grass between the Clubhouse and Golf Terrace. Happily, no one was injured."

Interestingly, in the same notes, the names of two famous golfers were mentioned – Sandy Herd and Harry Vardon. Apparently they had been "astonishing the Donegal natives" that week by some fine play at Rosapenna. Vardon had first visited Ulster some 15 years earlier when "in a great professional tournament" at Royal Portush he was beaten by Herd on the final hole.

It was at Royal Portrush that Herd had set out on his distinguished professional career – he had been appointed Club professional in 1890, his first professional appointment. He was recommended for the post by one of the all-time golfing greats, Tom Morris, known as the "grand old man of golf," who also had an interesting link with Royal Portrush, having helped with the lay-out and design of the course.

In that old tournament, Morris was Herd's caddy and mentor and together they were a formidable team. One report of the match mentioned the fact that Morris was not too keen on Sunday golf, recalling what he had once said to two English players on the subject: "If you twa gentlemen dinna need a rest on the Sabbath, the links does." An amusing story is also told of Morris when he met Andrew Carnegie who was in St. Andrews to

The famous Fifth Green.

receive the freedom of the city. They had a long conversation and at the conclusion, Carnegie gave Tom his card, on which he had written on the back: "Tom Morris, king of golfdom, your loyal subject. A.C."

The final paragraph from another report on that professional tournament over the Portrush links gives a great insight into the character of old Tom Morris: "Herd's match with Vardon was very keenly contested, having only been won on the last green. When the two players came to the penultimate green Herd's ball was found lying about six feet from the hole, while his opponent had played the odd and lay dead. Scarcely a word had been exchanged between Herd and Morris all the way round, but the latter now walked solemnly forward, lifted the flag, and with a stern look at Herd, said, 'Saundy, there's the hole.' Sandy did as his old master suggested and holed the ball."

In those days Vardon was something of a legend in the realms of golf, having won the Open championship no fewer than six times. He was also the first British player to win the US Open.

Sandy Herd, a Scotsman, had won the British Open in 1902. In August of that year he was back in Portrush playing an exhibition match on the Royal Portrush links. "Herd was seen at his very best," it was reported in a leading golf magazine. "He could hardly, it seemed, do anything wrong and, in addition to great brilliance, his play was marked by marvellous consistency. His splendid total of 70 establishes a new record for the course, a record which, if I mistake not, will take a deal of beating."

The great Harry Vardon in action.

A big gallery of spectators watched the match and among the crowd was another prominent golfer of the day. The same correspondent wrote: "It is interesting to note that the most prominent lady golfer of the day was also on the Portrush links on Saturday. I allude to Miss May Hezlet, the ladies' open champion who, it was noticed, followed the course of the play with keen interest."

-MARRIE McALEESE-

greatest golfing family

*"...in those halcyon days, Portrush occupied
a unique position in the world of ladies' golf."*

Portrush had its own golfing superstar in those early years of the last century, a young lady called May Hezlet – she was regarded as one of the top lady golfers in the world, having won the Ladies' Open Championship no fewer than three times as well as numerous other top-ranking competitions.

Her sister, Florence, was also no mean golfer – on one occasion they competed in the final of the Ladies Golfing Championship at Newcastle with May coming out on top. According to one sports writer of the day, the two sisters had created a unique record in the history of golf by contesting that Championship final. The Royal Portrush Club was so proud of their achievements that the ladies were to have their portraits painted and placed in the gentlemen's clubhouse.

"It is questionable if Miss May Hezlet has yet an equal in the ladies' golfing world; certainly she has no superior, and the proposal of the Golf Club will be heartily approved by all golfers throughout the United Kingdom."

Having their portraits placed in the gentlemen's clubhouse, no less! I'm sure the sisters, who probably could have outplayed most of the men, would have been suitably impressed!

A writer in "Ladies Golf," one of the most influential golf magazines of the day, had this to say: "The greatest of the golfing families among the ladies is without doubt that of the Hezlets. It is one of the curiosities of golf that for four successive years the sisters, Miss May and Miss Florence Hezlet, who are now Mrs Ross and Mrs Cramsie, opposed each other in the final of one or two of the national championships. Miss May held the Ladies Championship for three years, and in the Irish championship she was victorious five times."

No mention was made of another Hezlet sister, Violet, who was also no mean golfer. In May, 1911, she reached the final of the Ladies Open Championship at Royal Portrush, being only narrowly beaten by Canadian golfer Dorothy Campbell, who was then holder of the United States and Canadian ladies championships. She had also won the British championship in 1911. It was Violet's first appearance in a major championship final and it was no disgrace to be beaten by such a strong opponent.

In 1902 May Hezlet was the ladies open golf champion and she offered some sound advice to youngsters on the finer points of the game in an article she wrote for "Girls Realm" magazine: "All girls can play golf well if only they set about it in the right way and the younger they begin the better it is for their style. The best plan is to watch closely some really good

Straight down the middle.

amateurs or professionals playing, and to copy their swings as much as possible, but with certain modifications which may suit one's own style the better.

"Above all, swing naturally. Half-an-hour's practice at swinging will do more good than a couple of hours pouring over books and trying to play by rule. 'Keep your eye on the ball' is the chief rule to remember, and next in importance comes 'slow back.' This latter maxim, it is pointed out, does not mean, as some people think, that the club is to be lifted up as if it were a ton weight, but only that in comparison the upward swing must be slower than the downward.

"Watching professionals play, the beginner will see hardly any difference between the upward and downward swings, and will stand aghast at the quickness with which they hit; but in reality the upward swing is always a little slower than the downward, as it gives more certainty to the stroke being a well-hit one."

There were two other members of the Hezlet family who were no mean golfers either – Mrs Hezlet and her other daughter, Emily. On one occasion which must surely be unique in the annals of golf, Mrs Hezlet and her four daughters played a match against a team of top players representing the Ladies Branch – and the Hezlets won comfortably!

There is no doubt that in those halcyon days, Portrush occupied a unique position in the world of ladies' golf and not only because of the brilliant Hezlet sisters. Miss Rhona Adair could hold her own with any of the Hezlets -she had won the Ladies Championship in 1900. Three years later, writing in a leading golf magazine, a correspondent noted that "the players who stand at the head of ladies golf in the Kingdom are two members of the Portrush Club – Miss May Hezlet and Miss Rhona Adair, who may often be seen playing on the Portrush course."

It went on: "Miss Rhona Adair was champion three years ago, and Miss May Hezlet now holds the coveted trophy for the second time. Let us hope that she or Miss Adair will win it again next week and that the handsome trophy will be retained in Ireland for the fourth year." The championship was played on the Portrush links and the victor was Miss Adair.

To commemorate her great achievement in 1899 at Newcastle when she won both the Irish and United Kingdom championships another portrait was commissioned and it was officially handed over in April, 1900.

"The portrait of Miss May Hezlet, the lady champion of the United Kingdom, which was last year subscribed for by members of the Royal Portrush Golf Club, was formally presented to the Ladies' Branch of the club on Monday afternoon," it was reported in the local Press.

The date was April 16, 1900 and the portrait commemorates her stunning achievement the previous year. It still hangs today in the Ladies' Branch clubhouse. It was painted by Harry R. Douglas, one of Northern Ireland's finest portrait painters "and the artistic result is all that could be desired."

The unveiling ceremony was a sedate affair. Afternoon tea was served and afterwards (perhaps they were not invited for tea) "a few members of the gentlemen's club attended for the purpose of formally handing over the portrait."

As a golfer, May Hezlet was seldom out of the headlines, but some years later, in 1908, she made headlines off the golf course when she got married to the Rector of Portrush, the Rev. Arthur E. Ross.

The wedding, as you can imagine, was a very stylish affair with distinguished guests coming from far and near – it was one of the few occasions when "May" was given her proper title – Mary Elizabeth Linzee Hezlet. She was the second daughter of Colonel and Mrs Hezlet of Bovagh.

Huge crowds gathered outside Aghadowey Parish Church to catch a glimpse of the bride and groom.

An extensive account of the ceremony appeared in The Constitution (the editor and his wife were among the guests) which reported: "The bride is more widely known as Miss May Hezlet, the most distinguished member of a distinguished golfing family, who has placed to her credit a roll of victories on the links such as no other lady golfer can lay claim to."

There was a word of praise, too, for the bridegroom: "The Rev. A.E. Ross, who is one of the most zealous and cultured among the younger clergymen of the Church of Ireland, has for the last six years discharged with much acceptance the duties of Rector of Portrush, and no one is more highly respected in the popular watering place."

A special train had been laid on to convey many of the guests from Coleraine to the station at Aghadowey "where brakes and other vehicles were in readiness to convey the visitors to Aghadowey Church." Many others had driven from Portrush, Coleraine and Ballymoney by motor cars and other conveyances. After the ceremony a reception was held in a large marquee erected in the grounds of the family home, Bovagh House.

In addition to a report of the wedding, *The Constitution* carried a comprehensive list of the wedding presents and the names of the donors. There was also a list of all who had attended. One of the more unusual presents listed was a case of gold safety pins and there were several blotters – the biro had not been thought of then!

It seems appropriate to end with a few lines of advice to young ladies aspiring to the game of golf penned by the great lady herself. She wrote in 1904: "It is now generally acknowledged that golf is the game – par excellence – for women. The girl of the present day must have some outlet for her superfluous energy, and she is not contented with the life which women were expected to lead in former years. In those days their principal occupations were household duties, and sewing or embroidery. Exercise was not considered needful, and a quiet walk in the garden was the only change permitted from the work-chamber or still room. Household duties are a very necessary part of life, and sewing and amusements of the like nature are excellent in moderation, but they are not enough to satisfy the tastes of the modern girl. Exercise in the open-air is a necessity to her, and when combined with healthful bodily exertion, so much the better."

historic trip to the causeway

·MAURICE MCALEESE·

"Captain Wysner…was the first to carry his steamer, the 'Britannia,' on a pleasure trip from the Clyde to the Giant's Causeway."

It is believed that the first organised cruise or "pleasure trip" to the Giant's Causeway by passenger steamer took place at the beginning of the nineteenth century when the vessel "Britannia" set sail from the Clyde in Scotland. That historic voyage was recalled a century or so later when the amalgamation of two great steamship companies, the Ayr-Laird lines, was announced.

There was speculation at the time as to which name the new company would adopt but, as one shipping journal noted, "the Laird line have probably the stronger claim…because although not so well known in Belfast, in ports like Larne, Coleraine, Portrush, Londonderry, Sligo, Westport and Dublin, a good many of the traders are shareholders." The Laird line was believed to be the oldest steamship owners in the United Kingdom, so the claim to predominance was strong. However, old records are not too clear as to how long the Laird line was in the shipping trade or what connection it had to Ireland prior to 1814.

A notice which appeared in a Glasgow shipping journal in 1851 announcing the death of a Captain Wysner gives a clue. It states: "Captain Wysner, whose decease is announced, was the first to carry his steamer, the 'Britannia,' on a pleasure trip from the Clyde to the Giant's Causeway with a distinguished party." The sight of the large steamer, spewing clouds of smoke into the atmosphere as it came within sight of the Ulster coastline aroused huge interest and excitement for thousands of inhabitants and sightseers. This is how it was described in that old journal: "The astonished inhabitants in their thousands crowded the hills and promontories all along the shores of Antrim to see a ship with a smoking funnel and a band of music on board, sailing against wind and tide." It was out of this historic pleasure trip that a lucrative trade developed between ports of the Clyde and the North of Ireland "from which great advantages have unquestionably arisen to the inhabitants of both kingdoms."

The Britannia had been built in 1812; she had a gross tonnage of just 73 tons and before crossing the Channel on her maiden pleasure trip to the Causeway, she had been carrying passengers and cargo between various ports on the Clyde.

"In those far off days when the steamboat service was in its infancy," it was noted, "it will be seen from advertisements that season tickets were granted and family parties carried at reduced fares, which other carrying companies have more recently adopted."

It is believed that the passenger trips to the Causeway continued for a couple of seasons and that many people took the opportunity to view the stunning Causeway headlands from the comfortable decks of this old steamship.

Coming back to the beginning of the twentieth century, it was possible to take a mini cruise to the Causeway from Portrush and many holidaymakers did so, most of them viewing the great headlands from the deck of a ship for the first time. One of these was the passenger steamer "Gardenia" which, in the summer of 1902, was operating daily pleasure trips along the coastline. The trips catered for large numbers of tourists and were mostly to Carnlough, Rathlin, Port Ellen (Islay), Culdaff Bay and Moville.

Another short trip was from Portrush to Moville and this was by the paddle steamer "Cynthia" which operated in and out of Portrush harbour for quite a few summers.

In 1904 pleasure cruises were also in vogue, thanks to the local representative of the Laird Line, Mr. James C. Caldwell. It was reported that he had arranged for a series of short pleasure cruises by the Laird Line steamers. The first of these was to Derry and the second to Larne, and this was followed by shorter trips around Sheep Island – according to the Press "those who availed themselves of the trips speak in glowing terms of their delightful nature." Other trips were being arranged and should provide "an admirable means of spending a day or an afternoon." It was further pointed out: "Civility, courtesy, and a desire to please go a long way in a tourist's or traveller's estimation, and no lack of these will be found on Laird's boats.

The ss. Rose of the Laird Line brought some hundreds of excursionists from Rothesay on Monday who, after enjoying the sights of Portrush for a few hours, returned to the Clyde watering-place the same afternoon."

During the Victorian era, local fishermen operated their own boat excursions from the Causeway around the famous headlands and many visitors took the opportunity of a short sea trip, usually in a small open rowing boat. Some of the boatmen ventured into the mouth of the gaping Portcoon Cave which was spectacular enough but on many occasions the excitement would be heightened by the discharge of a shotgun into the depths of the cave – the idea was to produce a thundering echo, adding to the overall experience. The noise was probably ringing in their ears for a long time afterwards!

Anyone making the trip today would probably have to forego that particular experience because discharging a shotgun inside the cave would probably result in a prosecution of some kind and confiscation of the firearm!

Portcoon Cave.

Tourists coming to Portrush from Scotland on board the passenger steamship "Hazel" or any of the other Laird liners, would have had a sneak preview of the Causeway headlands while skirting the coastline on their way to Portrush. A writer in the "Glasgow Evening News" had this to say: "The Laird Line have practically discovered Portrush to us in the West of Scotland for in arranging a swift daily service they have put tedium out of count, and a voyage that in ordinary circumstances might have proved slow and somewhat tiresome, is now an exhilaration." He went on to stress that "with every attention given to the comfort of passengers and the most beautiful scenery in both countries close on view from one port is left till another is reached, is there anything nearer perfection that the tourist could want?"

When the new daylight service between Portrush and Ardrossan was being inaugurated in June, 1907 it opened up a new day excursion for the holiday public. The scenery on the route was "of more than ordinary interest" with the vessel close to land during the whole voyage. It was pointed out that en route the steamer passed the Island of Arran, Sands Island, Mull of

Kintyre, Rathlin Island, Fair Head, Carrick-a-Rede, Ballycastle, the Giant's Causeway, and the ruins of Dunluce Castle.

The scenery is certainly breathtaking and it is nicely summed up in these little verses penned by an unknown poet of 100 years ago:

I stood upon Ramore Head
And gazed on such a scene!
The ocean lay before me,
Bathed in a sunny sheen.

To westward Derry's coastline
Beyond bold Donegal;
Then further out north-eastward
Lay islands great and small.

Till once again I saw the coast
Of Erin bold and grand;
Fair Head stood out a sentinel
The ocean to withstand.

The Giant's Causeway met my view,
Dunluce both stern and grey;
The White Rocks then in garments pure,
Beyond their stretch of bay.

And here beneath Ramore's great head-
Right here beneath my feet-
Portrush lay bathed in purest air,
A healthful, sweet retreat.

- MAURICE McALEESE -

george bernard shaw at the causeway

*"he expressed himself as highly delighted
with its wonderful geological formation."*

I n the old days, a holiday in Portrush would not have been complete
without a visit to the Giant's Causeway, probably by way of the old
Causeway tram, and for many visitors the only way to see the stunning
headlands properly was by taking to the sea.

Local fishermen operated boat trips from tiny Brenther harbour, just a short
walk from the entrance to the Causeway, and they also acted as guides,
displaying a store of knowledge acquired over many years, the bulk of their
stories, usually a mixture of myth and folklore, passed down from one
generation to the next.

Brenther harbour is not really a harbour as such, more a rocky inlet with no
proper jetty or landing place – old photographs show lines of rowing boats
hauled up on the rocky shoreline.

Embarking and disembarking must have presented quite a challenge for
passengers but it all added, I'm sure, to the excitement and adventure for
those brave enough to take to the waves. Doubtless the experience was a
highlight for many thousands of visitors over the years.

The sound of gunfire was probably the last thing people expected to hear
when being rowed around the Causeway. But that frequently happened

when boats arrived at the mouth of the gaping Portcoon Cave, one of the many caves along this part of the coastline.

At a given signal, a marksman previously positioned on a ledge nearby, would discharge a shotgun, the thundering echo reverberating inside the cave, the intention being to enhance still further the thrill and experience for tourists. Depending on the mood of the boatman-guide, they may or may not have been warned of the impending bang.

Those old boat trips – the boats were mostly drontheims, sometimes also known as Norway yawls – have now been consigned to history. One reason advanced for their demise towards the middle of the last century was that with the modern pace of living, even for those on holiday and even in those days, there just was not enough time for tourists to explore the Causeway on foot and take a boat trip as well.

The vessels survived as fishing boats well into the twentieth century, and they were a common sight in and around small coves and harbours along the Donegal and Antrim coasts, as well as on the Scottish island of Islay. Today many people who visit the Causeway walk past the tiny Brenther harbour unaware of its interesting history and its link with a more leisurely era. Perhaps the time has come to think about reviving the Causeway boat trips, particularly in view of the planned improvements soon to be undertaken at the World Heritage site.

I wonder if George Bernard Shaw, who visited the Causeway in the early part of the last century, took one of those boat trips around the headlands? If he did, no mention was made of it in the Press reports of his visit. Described as "the famous playwright, socialist and sociologist," he had arrived at the Causeway one Sunday morning, having "motored thither" from Belfast, crossing from Heysham the previous night.

The report continued: "Accompanied by Mrs Shaw, he inspected the Causeway, and expressed himself as highly delighted with its wonderful geological formation, as also with the coast scenery of the district. During his sojourn at the Causeway Hotel he neither said nor did any of the disconcerting things for which he is notorious; rather, he gave the impression of a shy, retiring man who preferred to retail his ideas to a grateful public at so much a time, and, of course, he adhered strictly to the vegetarian diet which he prescribes in and out of season. On Monday morning Mr. Shaw left for Kilrea, where he dined at the Mercer's Hotel, and afterwards proceeded to Belfast. Possibly he will embody his impressions of this part of the country in one of his future plays, or, better still, prefaces. If so, they will make piquant reading."

It would seem that Mr. Shaw also missed the opportunity during his short visit to take a trip on the Causeway tram to Portrush, an experience he would no doubt have thoroughly enjoyed and one which might well have inspired him to feature the old tram in one of his future plays – an "Orient Express" type of thriller, perhaps!

A famous American preacher, the Rev. De Witt Talmage, definitely did take one of the boat trips during his Causeway visit and he later wrote memorably about it, which is not surprising because it was said of him that "his fluency and the picturesqueness of his language and imagery were remarkable."

Here he describes his feelings on entering Runkerry Cave: "As the boat surges into this cavern you look around, wondering whether there are enough oarsmen to manage it. A man fires a pistol that we may hear the report, as loud in that cavern as the heaviest crash of an August thunderstorm. You swing round for a few moments in that strange temple, and then come forth with an impression that you will carry forever. There can be no power in time or eternity to efface that stupendous memory. The rustic guides talk to you with the ease of a geologist about felspar and hornblende and basalt and trap-rock."

The Rev. De Witt Talmage - a famous Causeway visitor.

This reverend gentleman, the most famous preacher of his day in America, was mightily impressed with his visit to the Causeway. "You go to look at a celebrated lake, but you have seen other lakes. You go to look at a high mountain, but you have seen other mountains. You go to see a great city, but you have seen other cities. You go to see a famous tree, but you have seen other trees. But there is nothing in the world like the Giant's Causeway. It stands alone and aside from all geological wonders. There is no canvas high enough, no pencil skilful enough, no genius mighty enough, to adequately present this curiosity. Ireland might well have been built if for nothing but to hold the Giant's Causeway."

There is more than a hint of this great Presbyterian clergyman's preaching skills in his final paragraph: "After the

153

roof of the world has fallen in and the capitals of the mountains shall have crumbled, and the foundations of the earth have sunk, these grey columns shall run their grandeur across the desolation, and these organ pipes of basalt sound forth the dirge of a dead and departed world."

Many visitors to the Causeway, of course, took the opportunity of visiting other well-known attractions and foremost among these was the rope bridge at Carrick-a-Rede near the village of Ballintoy. However, a discordant note was struck by one visitor from Liverpool who, in a letter to *The Constitution*, complained about visitors to the swinging bridge being "fleeced" as he put it.

He wrote: "The hotel proprietors and respectable residents of these localities should, however, set their faces against the practice of fleecing visitors which has become too common of late. For instance, a charge of 3d as 'toll for trespass' is now demanded by a farmer from each individual who would pass along the pathway from Ballintoy to see the swinging bridge. Upon inquiry, I find this is a recent imposition, which should not be paid, as a right-of-way has been established there, and that the owner of the estate knows nothing about such a practice and, if he did, would soon put an end to it. If such practices are allowed, Irish people need not be surprised if their tourist traffic does not flourish in their lovely country."

CARRICK-A-REDE ROPE BRIDGE -MAURICE McALEESE-

a little bit of hokey-pokey

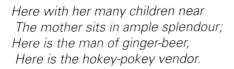

Here with her many children near
 The mother sits in ample splendour;
Here is the man of ginger-beer,
 Here is the hokey-pokey vendor.

-from an old poem, author unknown.

Ice cream vendors were a familiar sight on the streets of Portrush a hundred years ago, with their horse-drawn carts – there were also hand-carts pushed by the vendors - eye-catchingly painted to attract customers.

At the height of the season they did a brisk trade, selling the ice-cream in a variety of receptacles– the cone and the slider were still some way off in ice-cream technology. The description "ice-cream cones" was first used in 1909 and that happened in America; it heralded a new way of eating ice-cream. The Italians may have invented ice-cream but the inventor of the cone was a man called Ernest A. Hamwi, an American of Syrian descent.

The ice-cream which the vendors were selling in Portrush in those days was home-made and there were no restrictions or regulations in place concerning the contents or quality so there would have been quite a range of varieties and tastes and flavours to tickle the palette. Before the edible cone came along the ice-cream would have been sold in a small glass or taken away wrapped in paper – this became known by the name "hokey pokey" and it may well have given rise to the term "poke" which was also used to describe the cone.

The need for legislation to control the sale and manufacture of ice-cream was evident and it was put in place in April, 1903 when the Ice-Cream Act became law. It was badly needed, in fact, because some of the ice-cream being sold was often, according to some references, "of a poisonous nature."

That may have been somewhat exaggerated; nevertheless the same source claimed that the content of much of the ice-cream being sold by the street vendors was comprised of "deleterious" stuff. This, it was maintained, was due either to constituent elements or the unsanitary environment of the place of manufacture of the so-called "ice-cream."

A Press notice proclaimed: "Every vendor is obliged by the Act to have his name and address displayed legibly on his barrow, or if not trading under his own name, the address of the place of manufacture. This salutary regulation places an efficient instrument in the hands of sanitary inspectors for checking the manufacture of vile decoctions."

It was observed too that much energy was sometimes displayed by the authorities in detecting surplus water in buttermilk so the same energy should be expended in the analysis of ice-cream samples.

Just how many "vile decoctions" the sanitary inspectors would have detected in Portrush and what effect it had on the ice-cream vendors – not to mention their customers - is a matter for speculation but it probably meant that the simple pleasure of having a nice cool ice-cream on a hot summer day at the seaside was all the more enjoyable because of the quality assurance provided by the new legislation.

Although ice-cream was on the menu in some of the restaurants in Portrush, there was not an outlet specialising in ice-cream, what would be described today as an ice-cream parlour. About a year after the Ice Cream Act was introduced, in the summer of 1904, that was about to be rectified and, appropriately, because of their reputation in this particular line of business, it would happen through the enterprise of an Italian family.

In June of that year, the Forte brothers set up business in Portrush and to this day the name Forte (although there are different branches) is still very much associated with Portrush. In the advertising columns of *The Constitution* it was announced that "A. Forte Brothers", late of 23 Finsley Gate, Burnley and Padham, Lancashire had opened an establishment at Church Pass in Portrush. Under the headline "Ices" it revealed that they were vendors and makers of ice-cream for Bazaars, Balls, Tea Parties and Private Families. Makers to the Mayor of Burnley in 1895, '96, '97 and '99.

The Forte brothers also had branches at Main Street in Larne and Ann Street in Belfast. In addition to ice-cream they sold all kinds of pastry, mineral waters and high-class confectionery. You may depend upon the quality bearing the name of "A. Forte Brothers" was the parting shot in that old advertisement.

The Italian connection was quite strong in Portrush – the Morelli's, the Divito's, the Marsella's and the Forte's, of course, have had long and distinguished links with the town. In 1911 Peter Morelli, who already had shops in Coleraine and Portstewart, opened one in Portrush – today only the Morelli family still carry on business in the town, manufacturing ice-cream and maintaining the Italian catering link with the old days.

In those old days, the numerous ice-cream vendors in Portrush must have been complying with the new regulations pretty well because their numbers were not diminished and their carts, whether pushed or horse-drawn, remained very much part of the seaside scene. Sometimes accidents did happen, however. In the summer of 1913 a serious incident occurred when a horse drawing an ice-cream cart in Golf Terrace took fright and bolted.

It galloped down Eglinton Street where some men employed by the Tramway Company were working. They tried to stop the frightened animal but failed and it continued its wild run. And then an amazing thing happened. As the horse careered down Mark Street and was turning the corner at the Northern Counties Hotel, a young boy named Patrick Gallagher (he was just 12 years old) found himself directly in its path. He did not panic but "made a pluck" at the reins and managed to bring the runaway horse to a standstill. A Press report of the incident concluded: "The lad's action is to be complimented as had the horse made its way to the Main Street serious damage might have been done."

The horse careered down Mark Street.

Young Patrick was hero of the hour and no doubt he received an appropriate reward – and a big helping of ice-cream – from the grateful owner. And his father would have been a proud man too – he was Sergeant John Gallagher of the R.I.C. and he was in charge of the station in Portrush.

-MAURICE MCALEESE-

homeward bound

*"Suddenly the crowds on the pier and wharf
became silent and rapidly melted away."*

Holidays, like all good things, must come to an end and in Portrush a hundred years ago the departure of thousands of Scottish visitors who had spent what one writer described as "a really delightful time in Ulster," was frequently a noisy and colourful spectacle to behold. The scene is captured beautifully in a colourful description published in the The Constitution under the headline "Homeward Bound."

It painted a lively, sometimes moving, sometimes humorous, picture of the departure scenes at the harbour as holidaymakers thronged the quayside to board the "Hazel."

It was the end of August, 1913 and the reporter caught the atmosphere splendidly with a few deft strokes of the pen: "Except on one day, glorious weather favoured their annual sojourn away from the toils and noises of city life. Hot sunshine from a pearly sky beamed on their departure; the sea glittered grey, with hardly a ripple; and a thin haze hung over the distant water, obscuring all but a fragment of the bluff outline of Donegal."

It's easy to imagine the animated scenes at the harbour as the Scottish visitors took their leave and we are told that they were "a good humoured crowd" and that confetti was flying in all directions. It was explained: "There was no wedding party so far as one could see, but in these latter days it

All aboard the "Scotch Boat"

appears to have become the custom for these young Scotch people to pelt each other with confetti on such occasions in token, presumably, of close friendship and sometimes of affection."

The confetti was often a lasting reminder, at least until home was reached, because, as the article pointed out, it would often slip down between the collar and the neck, to be remembered throughout the day.

A large section of the departing crowd had arrived in Portrush from other parts of the Province by rail and road to catch the ferry and they had to be on the quayside about an hour or so before the boat sailed. It must have seemed like a mass exodus as they made their way down to the harbour: "Heavily laden jaunting cars, men and women carrying trunks and other holiday impedimenta, young women in their brightest attire sweet-hearting with bare-headed young men, poured down Kerr Street in a continuous stream. Perhaps one half of them went on board the Hazel, the rest – mostly their own country folks, had only come down to the quayside to see them off – 'safely out of Ireland' as one facetiously expressed it."

They were in a happy mood because waves of singing echoed up and down the quayside until it was shattered by a sound which must have been heard in every street and laneway in Portrush – the deafening blast of the Hazel's steam horn warning that the ship would soon be casting off. It had the desired effect: "Young folks pressed through the crowd to the gangways; laughing girls flicked the confetti from their hair and bosoms; young men flung it back on them from their hats; and there were hurried partings, a few paternal, some filial, but mostly mixed. Yet some of them were not hurried, for one young fellow returned and had a second kiss before he sprang across the gangway."

Under the command of Captain Hately, directing operations from the bridge, the Hazel cast off, passengers crowding the decks, waving a last farewell to Portrush and the friends they were leaving behind.

There is something almost poetic in this description of the Hazel finally pulling away from Portrush: "But for age as well as youth, the Irish holiday of 1913 had come to an end. Hawsers were unfastened, the captain appeared on the bridge, and the ship cast off into mid-water. Then afloat and ashore there was a simultaneous fluttering of handkerchiefs and favours of many colours. The Hazel, thronged above and below from stem to stern, looked like a huge moving basket of waving flowers. Song answered song, cheers were exchanged, and as the dense smoke poured from her funnel the good ship, with her freight of merry home-goers, passed out into the shining sea. Suddenly the crowds on pier and wharf became silent and rapidly melted away."

Of course, the Hazel was not the only vessel on the route between Portrush and Ardrossan – two others were the "Olive" and the "Lily" and along with the Hazel they made up a fine trio of the Laird fleet.

On another occasion, this was the scene as the Hazel and the Lily prepared for departure: "Friends from the other side who had the good fortune to be able to remain in dear old Erin for a few days longer bade a temporary adieu, while natives of the Emerald Isle took farewell of acquaintances which they had formed amongst the folk from the land of the thistle.

"The steamers gracefully glided out of the harbour, alive with fluttering headgear and handkerchiefs, the salutations being returned by the large crowds on the quay and south pier. The steamers passed round Ramore Head, and soon faded away in the distance. Most of the gay holidaymakers from the Scottish city had thus taken their departure. We would fain keep them with us a little longer but can only look forward to meeting them again next year, when they will be, as ever, welcome to old Ireland."

on the threshold of a golden age

I imagined I could hear old sea voices coming from some mystical shore.

T he slow sad murmur of distant seas… is a line in James Stephens' poem, "The Shell," and like him, I too, have heard something that sounded like the slow sad murmur of distant seas when, as a young boy growing up in Portrush, I would press a shell to my ear while walking or playing on the broad sweep of the East Strand.

Sometimes, in the mysterious swish and swirl of those distant, shell-bound oceans, I imagined I could hear old sea voices coming from some mystical shore. It was always a bit exasperating because I could never really determine what they were saying or trying to say. As I've discovered in putting together this book, there are other "shells" for that purpose; I've been lucky enough to find some of them and all I've had to do is listen – from a distance.

So I thought it would be nice to listen to some of the voices from the last summer of the nineteenth century in Portrush, the beginning of the end of the Victorian era, you could say, when Portrush was poised not only on the threshold of a new century but on the threshold also of a new and exciting "golden age" in its remarkable seaside history.

Without putting too much of a spin on it, I discovered that in the summer of 1899, the humble bicycle was the most popular mode of transport on the streets of Portrush, so much so that a fine new cycle park had been provided right in the centre of the town capable of holding upwards of 100 bicycles.

A cycling craze had taken hold of visitors and residents alike and it was giving rise to problems – concern was being expressed as to the manner in which some of the bicycles were being ridden. In August of that summer, it was noted in the "Seaside Jottings" column of *The Constitution*:

"Now that the evenings are rapidly lengthening, the danger arising from cycling without lamps is being increasingly felt. It is unsafe almost to cross the street owing to the large number of cyclists of both sexes whisking past without lights, and often without any warning of their approach, for the bell is generally rung when the pedestrian is within a few feet of the advancing wheel. It is now too late, we presume, to make regulations for this season, but the time has come when the Urban Council must interfere. The use of lights after sundown should and indeed must be insisted upon. It is manifestly a protection which the local authorities owe to the public."

Some light relief was brought to the problem by the railway authorities who had erected two handsome lamps in front of the railway station and they were lit every evening. It was reported:
"Heretofore the outer entrance or approach to the station has often been very difficult after dark, but it is now beautifully illuminated, so that no trouble should be at any time after sundown experienced in traversing the space between the station and the Town Hall."

A traffic-free day.

It was felt that the fine dry weather of that summer had been responsible for the increasing number of cyclists. "They are of all ages and all styles – some graceful, but the larger proportion otherwise." A wry comment on art and skill – and perhaps shape – of individual cyclists!

Just watching the passing parade of the cycling brigade had its own entertainment value and this was certainly provided by a youngster described as "the youngest cyclist ever seen in the district." He had been "scorching" up and down the streets. He was just four or five years old and apparently it was "a treat to watch the skilful way in which he handles his tiny bicycle."

It was due to the initiative of the railway company earlier that summer that cyclists had now been provided with special accommodation "for their wheels." The man responsible for this was Mr. B.D. Wise, the railway company's chief engineer who, "with characteristic forethought" had arranged to have a bicycle stand erected at the café side of the station. "It will provide space for about 100 bikes," it was announced, "for each of which a nominal charge will be made. The scores of cyclists who visit Portrush in the summer evenings will be glad to know that their machines may be left in safe keeping for an hour or two."

The only serious threat to the cyclists in Portrush at that time came from another popular mode of transport – the jaunting car. And in the summer time there were many and most of the jarvies or drivers took great pride in their cars and horses. An insight into just how particular they were was revealed that summer when about forty of them lined up for an impressive parade and inspection. It was all for the benefit of the local council which issued licences for the vehicles on an annual basis.

Waiting for a fare.

How the inspection was carried out is interesting. A meeting of the Urban Council in June of that year was adjourned "for the purpose of making the annual inspection of the licensed hackney cars."

A report of the proceedings noted: "Upwards of 40 magnificently equipped cars were drawn up in line in Mark Street, and the display is one which it is doubtful if it could be equalled in Ireland. The teams proved eminently satisfactory, and having made a circuit of the town, they were again drawn up in front of the Town Hall, when Mr. R. H. Gilmore, MRCVS, Coleraine and Mr. W. Gill, Cromore, again inspected them with a view to allocating prizes presented by the Council for the best equipped teams."

After what was described as a critical inspection the judges made the following awards: 1, Mr. W. McNeill; 2 and 3, Mr. Jas. D. Hunter; very highly commended, Mr. James Thompson; highly commended, Mr. James D. Hunter.

When the council meeting resumed, the chairman commented that the cars would compare favourably with those of most places. They might have one or two weeds, but he thought their hackney cars and horses were a credit to any place.

Mr. Gilmore, one of the judges, was also effusive in his praise. The parade, he said, was one of the finest that could be made in Ireland and he hoped their awards had given satisfaction not only to the car owners but to the public in general. His fellow judge, Mr. Gill, said it was a credit to any town that could turn out such teams. His hope that the parade would become an annual event, and that it would prosper, was greeted by applause.

Later that summer, one of the hackney cars was involved in an accident in which an old man had been knocked down. The victim, James McComb, was employed by the Tramway Company and the accident occurred in the course of his work which was to ring a bell for the purpose of warning pedestrians of the approaching tram at the corner of the Methodist Church.

This was a particularly sharp bend – the tram was coming from the railway station en route for the Causeway and a jaunting car, driven by John Peden, was coming down Main Street. A report of the incident continued: "As the two streets meet at a sharp angle, Peden was unable to observe the position of the tram, and thinking he had sufficient time to cross the tram lines in advance, the old man McComb, as the tram approached, moved backwards to the footpath, and in doing so the jaunting-car collided with him, knocking him down in front of the advancing engine and inflicting rather severe injuries to his head."

The driver of the tram was able to brake in time to avoid hitting the old man who was given medical attention by doctors at the scene and was later reported to be progressing favourably. The driver of the jaunting-car was arrested and later charged with negligently driving his car.

That accident happened shortly after the re-opening of the tramway using the overhead trolley system which had been opposed by the Urban Council. However, after lengthy legal wrangling, the tramway company had been given leave to introduce the new system and to mark the opening a "complimentary dinner" was given in the Causeway Hotel. It was hosted by Mr. William Acheson Traill and Mrs Traill and it was served, according to a Press report "in the usual recherché manner for which the Causeway Hotel cuisine is noted."

One of the highlights of the summer of 1899 in Portrush was due to one young lady who, in the space of just a couple of weeks, had made golfing history. She was hailed as a local heroine and huge crowds turned out to welcome her on her triumphant return. Her story is in the next chapter.

a great victory parade

*"…fire rockets were discharged
and a bonfire was lighted on the Salmon Green."*

There were amazing scenes of jubilation and celebration on the streets of Portrush one hot June night in the summer of 1899 – it seemed as if the entire population of the town had turned out and you could almost feel the high state of anticipation and excitement that hung in the warm night air.

What had brought such a vast number of people onto the streets and why had they gathered in a great concourse outside the railway station? What was all the excitement about? They were awaiting the arrival of a train carrying a very special passenger, a young lady who had taken the golfing world by storm – she had just brought off a unique double in the history of ladies golf by winning two major championships in the space of a couple of weeks.

The local heroine was Miss May Hezlet and as the train she and her mother were travelling in pulled slowly into the station the night sky was illuminated by an explosion of fireworks, surely a sound and a sight that left them in no doubt as to the type of welcome that awaited them.

The Portrush girl had won the Ladies Open Championship held under the auspices of the Ladies' Golfing Union of the United Kingdom, shortly after winning the Irish Ladies Open Championship, both played at Newcastle, making her, it was claimed, one of the youngest champions in the history of golf. Her double success received huge Press coverage: she was hailed by one writer as "a courageous and skilful player" and he added that her capture of the double crown was immensely popular.

In the open championship there had been a strong contingent of players from England and the Irish contestants were not expected to make much of an impact. As it turned out, eleven of the 25 Irish players in the field progressed to the third round; four reached the fourth round; three got through to the fifth and two to the semi-finals, both reaching the final – Miss Hezlet and Miss Magill, County Down, the reigning champion.

This is a brief description of the play: "The weather was magnificent, and there was a brilliant muster of spectators. Miss Hezlet was pretty closely held up to the eleventh hole, but the match was square at the thirteenth, and then she played steadily and brilliantly all the way home. She won the 14th, halved the 15th, won the 16th, and divided the 17th – thus winning the match and the open championship by 2 up and 1 to play."

In the final of the Irish Ladies Championship Miss Hezlet beat Miss Rhona Adair (Killymoon) 5 up and 4 to play.

It was a truly remarkable achievement and one which has probably never been equalled. At any rate, for Mary Elizabeth Linzee Hezlet (May) it was surely a dream come true and in the midst of that ecstatic welcome she must have been thinking back to the day when, as an eager eleven-year-old, she tried out her first set of golf clubs on the Royal Portrush links, probably under the watchful eye of her mother.

Even then she must have displayed some of the natural talent and flair that would take her to the pinnacle of success and ensure a place for her in the early annals of golfing history. Writing about her 1899 achievements, one golf correspondent observed: "Miss Hezlet has acquired wonderful judgement within a remarkably short period; and, aided by a strong physique, plays the game admirably in all its points. She was the runner-up in last year's Irish Ladies Golf Championship tournament at Malone and was only beaten by a putt on the last hole; while for some time past she has won most of the scratch medals offered by the Royal Portrush Club."

At the time she also held the record for the ladies' course at Portrush – 77. And she had gone round the tough men's course in 95 strokes.

When the sound of fireworks had died down that summer night in Portrush, a loud cheer went up as the young golfing star and her mother emerged from the railway station; they were greeted by a welcoming party which included leading members of the Royal Portrush Golf Club and she was presented with a large bouquet. Then, to the sound of a flute band from Coleraine, the pair were escorted to an open carriage drawn by four smart horses waiting in readiness just outside the station.

They were joined in the carriage by Colonel Pottinger and Mr. J.S. Alexander, D.L., of Royal Portrush but before the carriage moved off, there was a last-minute change of plan; horse-power was dispensed with. The horses were unhitched and "willing hands" pulled the carriage along Mark Street and Main Street to Rock Ryan, followed by the cheering crowds "and the band playing lively airs."

This is an extract from *The Constitution* report: "Opposite the Northern Counties Hotel, Colonel Pottinger, as Captain of the Club, on behalf of Miss Hezlet, thanked the people for the magnificent reception they had given her. At Rock Ryan fire rockets were again discharged, and a bonfire was lighted on the salmon green. Later in the evening, in the presence of a large crowd, Captain Watt, chairman of the Urban Council, in the name of the town, congratulated Miss Hezlet on the double victory she had won as a golfer, conferring distinction not only on herself but on Portrush and her country. Colonel Hezlet appropriately acknowledged the compliment."

It was surely a night to remember not only for May Hezlet and her family, but also for the crowds of residents and visitors. In keeping with the protocol of the times, no doubt, the young champion did not speak herself at that great reception, her father, Colonel Hezlet, and the Club Captain, doing so on her behalf. Perhaps her tender age had something to do with it as well – she was just 17 years old.

It was a truly remarkable achievement and one which has probably never been equalled.

Song of the dancing waves

Each wave, that we danced on at morning, ebbs from us,
And leaves us, at eve, on the bleak shore alone.

-Thomas Moore (I Saw From the Beach)

By and large, Portrush got a good Press as a holiday destination in the early summers of the last century. And all the singing of its praises, and there was quite a lot, seems to have been unsolicited – there does not appear to have been any great marketing strategy on the part of the town council. But that was about to change and with the setting up of a special advertising committee under the auspices of the Urban Council, a new emphasis would be put on the promotion of tourism as the new century beckoned.

Until then, promotion of tourism had been left largely to the railway and shipping companies. They were eager to promote their links with Portrush – every summer the trains brought many thousands of day-trippers and visitors to the town and the same was true of the Laird Line's passenger steamship service from Scotland.

This is the introduction to a report announcing the setting up of that old advertising committee: "In this advertising age the progressive businessman does not believe he has attained sufficient publicity by placing his name over his door. If you wish to attract the public you must advertise. In that magic word lies the secret of success, and the man who understands the art of skilful and judicious advertising need never feel the blighting pinch of impecuniosity."

Those who did not wish to experience "the blighting pinch of impecuniosity" must resort, it was suggested, "to some form or another of printer's ink" if they desired to win public favour.

With commendable foresight, the Portrush Advertising Committee had been set up for the purpose of raising funds in order to promote the charms and delights of Portrush as a seaside venue. And the Committee had made a good start, producing a large pictorial poster and a twenty page pamphlet for exhibition and circulation in Scotland and the North of England. The poster gave a beautiful bird's eye view of the town and surrounding coastline. It would be exhibited at hundreds of railway stations in Scotland and would also be posted at other stations in Manchester, Leeds, Liverpool and other North of England towns.

Ten thousand copies of the poster had been printed on high quality art paper and it was accompanied by a sketch map of the Antrim coast containing a selection of photographs of Portrush and the Giant's Causeway. It was reported that other forms of advertising had also been taken advantage of by the Committee and it was felt that the members had turned to excellent account the funds which had been placed at their disposal.

Portrush also had its own holiday newspaper – "The Portrush Weekly Programme and Visitors' Guide" – issued every Saturday and modestly priced at just one penny. It contained a summary of events for the ensuing week and carried a list of hotels, boarding-houses and private apartments. There were also sections giving visitors advice on where to go and what to see. It also carried quite a lot of advertisements which were inserted "at reasonable rates." It was on sale at Miss Woods, Bookseller and Stationer, Coleraine and Portrush.

Undoubtedly there would have been other items of interest in that old holiday newspaper and it would be fascinating to see a copy today but it is doubtful whether one exists. Anyway, here are a few extracts from other sources which give some idea of the lure and appeal of Portrush as a seaside resort in those old times:

The area of the town is about 211 acres, but of such a peculiar form that it possesses a seaboard of about two miles. Therefore, residence in the town itself may be fairly considered to hold out the advantages of life on board a ship, the Atlantic ocean beating practically all round – a sojourn, from this point of view, being as good as a sea voyage, without the latter's attendant inconveniences and other distressing accompaniments. Another feature is this, that the paths, streets and roads of Portrush dry up in an incredibly short time, even after the heaviest showers, this, of course, being due to the fact that the rain rapidly percolates through the sandy surface soil, and finds its way, either by flowing along over the sloping surface of the rock on which the town stands, or through the fissures in its mass, to the sea. This fact is of importance when it is remembered how beneficial it is for the young to be able to take exercise without running the risk of getting their feet wet, and also how necessary it is in cases of many invalids that they should be protected from the danger of walking or sitting on damp soil. Further, the exhausting effects of oppressive heat need never be experienced by any visitor on account of the prevalence of a refreshing sea breeze which is never absent even during the sultry weather of the dog days, on the extreme point of the headland called Ramore Hill.

- extract from a paper read by Dr. J.C. Martin, Portrush, at a meeting of the North of Ireland Branch of the British Medical Association in July, 1900.

The atmosphere at Portrush has been compared to that of the Riveria, and the sea on a fine day is well nigh as blue as the Mediterranean. The place is built upon a rather narrow promontory pushing out northwards into the Atlantic, and thus looking away across the mouth of Lough Foyle to the blue mountains of Donegal, with Malin Head in the distance, the other with the bold stretch of cliffs and headlands terminating in that basaltic marvel so grotesquely and ineptly named the Giant's Causeway, with the remoter cliffs of Rathlin Island as a background. That promontory is happily too rough and craggy towards its outer extremity to have tempted anyone to build upon it, and so Ramore Head has been preserved as one of the finest viewpoints in the world, and is a promenade of unequalled fascination.

-The Sheffield Weekly Telegraph, July, 1904.

Jaded townsfolk would do well to consider the claims of this famous watering-place. It is but a little over twelve hours journey from London, including two hours by sea, via Stranraer and Larne. The air is marvellously invigorating, and the breeze, sweeping in direct from the broad Atlantic, is peculiarly tonic in its effect. For attractions there is said to be, next to St. Andrews, the finest golf course in the British Islands. Dunluce Castle is a national heirloom of special interest to all lovers of the picturesque. Of the Giant's Causeway, nothing can be said that has not already been said about this wonder of the world. But the whole coast from Portrush to Fair Head is famous for its sights e.g., the White Rocks, the Giant's Head, the Lady's Wishing Arch, Dunluce, the Causeway Cliffs, Pleaskin Head, Carrick-a-Rede – all these are a joy forever. As for accommodation, all sorts can be had at very reasonable terms. There are many ways of going to Portrush from London, fares as low as 33s. return being available. The Midland route is said to be the most convenient.

- A letter published in London Opinion, June, 1904.

The attractions at Portrush are golf and sea bathing. The strand for ladies and children could not be excelled; there is salmon fishing on the Bush river, and an electric railway to the Giant's Causeway, the first constructed in the United Kingdom. This line runs along the highway, gives a good view of the headlands and cliffs, as well as Dunluce Castle, which has many interesting historical records.

At the Causeway there are two hotels; and here, in addition to examining the Grand Causeway, the visitor should walk along the headlands, from which a very fine view of the scenery may be obtained. The air on the seaboard of Ireland facing the Atlantic is highly charged with ozone, and more invigorating and healthful than any we know of elsewhere. Ozone is said to be produced by the action of the waves against the cliffs, by their being split into water dust, so that every sea cliff facing the Atlantic acts beneficially on the atmosphere and contributes to make our western seaboard such an ideal health resort. Derry may be visited in one day from Portrush, and its ancient historic walls and gates examined.

- Land and Water, October, 1902

Visitors to Portrush have remarked the effort that has been quietly made during the last few years to beautify the place with shrubs and flowers. Twenty years ago, or less, it was thought that nothing but coarse grass would grow at Portrush and hardly any attempt was made to grow anything. Portrush was regarded by the residents as a barren, arid bit of seashore which could be got to produce nothing in the guise of a blossom or a green leaf. Nothing but bent or wiregrass, it was concluded, could withstand the all prevailing sand and brine-laden winds. The bald peninsula and its vicinity was a sort of Aden, inhospitable alike to every form of flower, shrub or tree.

But we live and learn. It has been discovered that many plants and flowers, including a great variety of hardy annuals, grow well at Portrush, if a little care be taken to mix with the sand some good soil. There are a few plants and flowers which have been found to flourish in extremely poor ground. One of the former is a variety of the shrub Veronica, which was first introduced here, we believe from Bray, about 20 years ago. Veronica has made a home for itself in Portrush, and its very hardy, dull-leaved bushes are now to be seen all over the place. Another shrub which has found a footing here is Escallonia, its glossy leaves being much admired, but it is not quite so hardy as the Veronica. Among the hardy annuals which find sufficient nourishment in a poor sandy soil are Shirley Poppies, Pansies and Pinks. Wallflower also blooms in almost any situation.

-The Constitution, April, 1911.

These are just a few selections, chosen at random, and they illustrate the unique position which Portrush occupied in that golden age when its charms and delights were known and appreciated far beyond its shores, when the foundations were being laid for still greater things to come. But the song of the seaside would soon begin to sound like a dirge as the dark clouds of the Great War began to hover. And in the summer of 1915, although Portrush was still the mecca for thousands of holidaymakers and there was still "gaiety in the streets," there was nevertheless a perceptible change in the general atmosphere and outlook and as one commentary put it, "all is not gold that glitters this season."

It went on: "Those who know frown grimly at the universe, and aver that in the ordinary run of things there ought to be thousands more here. It is true that quite a number of southern people have, by force of circumstance, fled from their costly haunts overseas to Portrush, where they enjoy its magnificent sea, strands and cliffs, and are flourishing wonderfully in its tonic and stimulating air. But the visitors from Dublin and the south of

Ireland, welcome though they are, do not compensate for the normal influx from the prosperous sister island."

The loss of the cross-Channel passenger steamship link with Scotland, and with it the huge influx of Scottish visitors, was particularly felt and was seen as a severe blow not only to Portrush but the north coast generally.

That old commentary concluded with these prophetic words: "Truly, despite the gaiety and the throng, the times are out of joint, and joy will not again be unconfined until the thunders of the great guns have been quenched in an honourable and enduring peace."

It really was the end of a golden era. Portrush would never be the same again.

fair portrush

Dear Reeders – Wi' the kin' Editor's forebearance a wud like tae kin' o' kinomatigraff a few sober pictures o' the 'Brighton o' Irelan' as it appeared tae yours truly on last Setterday. Withoot a doot Portrush is aye there, wi' its Ramore Heid, twa strannie erms haudin' the bla'k rocks in the yin han' an' the white yins in the ither, the toon proper formin' its busy an' very weel proporshuned body, stretchin' its bare legs inlan' far ower the san' hills.

> "O' a' places touched by the sea
> Fair Portrush is the yin for me."

Cruel war an' its dreadful effects seem tae be fully realised even by the maist thochtless. The few canvalesent men in khaki wur revered almaist tae worship point. Al' man-made musick seems tae be on the rocks – wash'd aside by the incomin' tide, the strains o' which waves ir extremely weird indeed as they bring tae us the soun' o' money a dear voice noo still, the brave possessors o' which we'll no be likely tae meet in person again until "the sea gies up its deid."

Just let us dae oor duty on the lan' as weel as they did it on the water, an' we'll hae little tae be ashamed o' when peace is proclaimed. Had the city feythers an' mothers prohibited mixed moisterin' the famous place wud hae been bate. A diver's heart maun surely be weel set whan he can jump heid formist aff thon heichest rock at the Blue Pool an' go intae the boilin' surf wae a plunge that surprises ye ta see, then come tae the tap again, smal' wunner the crowd o' spectators gie them a bit o' applause.

As the train that waits on only a very big person, wus gan oot, an' the tide, which treats a' alike by waitin' on nane, wus comin' in, a wus compelled tae say guid-by fur the present, sweet and dearly beloved Portrush.

A.L.F.

(Northern Constitution, August 5, 1916).